Dancing on Air

*A Tale of Vengeance, Mercy, and
the End of the Death Penalty
in Newfoundland*

Eric Colbourne

BOULDER
PUBLICATIONS

Library and Archives Canada Cataloguing in Publication
Colbourne, Eric F. (Eric Freeman), 1944-, author
     Dancing on air : vengeance, mercy and the death penalty in Newfoundland
/ Eric Colbourne.

Includes index.
Previously published: Victoria, BC: FriesenPress, 2015.
ISBN 978-1-927099-82-7 (paperback)

     1. Capital punishment--Newfoundland and Labrador--History. 2. Trials
(Murder)--Newfoundland and Labrador--History. 3. Newfoundland and
Labrador--History. I. Title.
HV8699.C2C65 2016   364.3309718   C2016-901802-4

Published by Boulder Publications
Portugal Cove-St. Philip's, Newfoundland and Labrador
www.boulderpublications.ca

Design and layout: John Andrews
Editor: Stephanie Porter
Copy editor: Iona Bulgin

Printed in Canada

Newfoundland
Labrador

We acknowledge the financial support of the Government of
Newfoundland and Labrador through the Department of Tourism,
Culture and Recreation.

We acknowledge the financial support for our publishing program by the Government
of Canada and the Department of Canadian Heritage through the Canada Book Fund.

for Josephine and Dorothea

It is sweet to dance to violins
When life and love are fair:
To dance to flutes, to dance to lutes
Is delicate and rare:
But it is not sweet with nimble feet
To dance upon the air!

—Oscar Wilde,
The Ballad of Reading Gaol

Acknowledgements

One day in 1975, when I was a student at the University of Reading in England, my wife and I visited the historic Reading Gaol, where the great Irish writer Oscar Wilde penned one of the most famous ballads in English literature during his imprisonment in 1897. *The Ballad of Reading Gaol* tells the story of the 1897 hanging of a young trooper in the Horse Guards, Charles Wooldridge, for killing his young wife, Laura, in a fit of jealous rage. My visit to Reading Gaol and the tale of Trooper Wooldridge became the inspiration for this book.

Dancing on Air details two controversial murder cases that occurred in Newfoundland during the turbulent decade of the 1940s. The legal outcomes of both cases became significant milestones in the administration of justice in Canada.

Primary sources provide the substance of these two stories. These sources include the original trial transcripts and exhibits from the Supreme Court of Newfoundland and Labrador. Special thanks to Dawn Kieley, manager of Information Services at the Supreme Court, for providing access to key documents, some of which had not been opened since the trials concluded many decades ago.

The Rooms Provincial Archives deserves much of the credit for making a work of non-fiction like this possible. Their extensive holdings include the correspondence of the Commission of Government for Newfoundland, which provided vital details for the story.

The same must be said of the staff of the A.C. Hunter Public Library in St. John's who provided me with access to their collection of historic newspapers including the *Daily News*, *Evening Telegram*, *Twillingate Sun*, and *Grand Falls Advertiser*.

Paul Butler offered excellent advice on the organization of the manuscript.

Captain Dave Harvey of Her Majesty's Penitentiary facilitated access to several original documents which otherwise I would not have seen.

Some family members of those involved in the events provided details which added emotion and life to the narrative. Out of privacy concerns, they did not wish to be acknowledged but deserve special thanks for their contribution.

Two years ago the Hon. Susan Stride agreed to provide information about her grandfather, Sir Gordon Macdonald. Her assistance proved invaluable in helping me put a face to the man who became our last governor.

My wife, Marilyn, deserves special credit for assisting with the research.

One

Now, sir, hanging is clean. It's the cleanest way of all of putting them away, it's English—as English as cricket, or plum pudding, or Worcester Sauce.

—John Ellis, Britain's official hangman,
1899–1924

The massive stone outcrop of Gibbet Hill rising nearly 400 feet above sea level offers a commanding view of St. John's Harbour, the older downtown parts of the city, and the Waterford Valley to the west. In the spring of 1942, the fortified hill with its 155-millimetre guns guarded the entrance to a busy port filled with merchant ships, corvettes, and destroyer escorts. The few small coastal schooners seemed out of place amidst the ships of war.

Soldiers manning the site saw, immediately below them, the military camps near Deadman's Pond. Off to the northeast the Basilica of St. John the Baptist dominated the ridgeline overlooking the city. In the downtown area the four-faced clock tower of the Supreme Court Building rose prominently over the drab buildings around it.

On the warm afternoon of April 28, 1942, bright sunlight streamed through the vaulted windows in the main courtroom of the imposing building at 309 Duckworth Street. During the mid-afternoon break in the murder trial, a rush of spectators packed the available seats behind the prisoner's box. Some were curious onlookers driven by the lurid reports of the crime; others were reporters for the *Daily News* and the *Evening Telegram* hurriedly noting the details of the case for the next day's papers; and others wore the black frocks of clergymen.

The jury returned to the chamber at 4:45 p.m. Other than a muffled cough from someone in the crowded gallery, the courtroom was deathly quiet as the 12 men shuffled to their seats.

"Gentlemen of the jury, have you reached a verdict?" asked the chief justice, Sir William Henry Horwood of the Supreme Court of Newfoundland.

"We find the prisoner guilty," replied the jury foreman. He handed the clerk of the court the jury's handwritten decision.

"The prisoner will stand," Horwood instructed. "Herbert Augustus Spratt, you have been found guilty of the crime of murder. Do you have any reason why the sentence of this court should not be passed upon you?"

The accused remained silent as the chief justice asked the question a second time.

Horwood began his sentencing just a few minutes later, at 4:57 p.m.: "This court doth ordain you, Herbert Augustus Spratt, to be taken hence to the place from whence you came." The chief justice took another 30 seconds to deliver the full sentence, but it is likely the accused heard only the final and most dreaded of words, "and that you be there hanged by the neck." The young man flinched and stumbled backward in the prisoner's box.

Chief Justice Horwood's decision was firmly rooted in English criminal law under a statute known as *The Offences against the Person Act*, which received Royal Assent in 1861, of which clause two was unmistakeable in its intent: *Upon every Conviction for Murder the Court shall pronounce Sentence of Death.*

The penalty of death had been liberally applied in the old country for many hundreds of years prior to 1861. In the period between 1735 and 1860, for which there are reliable records, 11,000 executions, most by hanging, had been carried out in Great Britain. Until the mid-1800s, some 200 offences were regarded as capital crimes, which carried the death penalty. In the 21st century most of these offences seem absurd.

John Dean, variously described in the records as a child of eight or nine, may have been the youngest to suffer death by hanging. On February 23, 1629, he was convicted of arson at Abington, England, for setting fire to two barns in the town of Winsor. The judge saw evidence of wickedness in the boy's actions, which led directly to his death sentence.

In early August 1814, William Potter received the death penalty at the high court in Chelmsford, England, for damaging an orchard. He had chopped down an old apple tree for firewood. At his trial, Potter pleaded ignorance of the law, but to no avail. The judge had second thoughts several days after sentencing Potter but the wheels of justice were already in motion and he was hanged on August 12.

Until the latter half of the 19th century, these hangings were public events attended by large numbers of spectators, including men, women, and children, many dressed in their finest clothing. Some used the opportunity to voice their opposition to the execution, others came simply to witness the grisly spectacle of a dying man gyrating and kicking at the end of a rope, often referred to at the time as "Dancing on Air."

Many 19th-century laws on capital punishment remained in place for well over another 100 years in the United Kingdom and formed the basis for similar laws in all of the overseas territories linked to the mother country, including those which later came together as the Dominion of Canada.

The west coast of Canada experienced the introduction of British criminal law around 1849 with the founding of the crown colony of Vancouver Island. Unfortunately, until the second quarter of the 20th century, the scales of justice in this colony, and in what later became British Columbia, invariably tilted against Aboriginal and other minority prisoners, most of whom were unrepresented in the courtroom and did not understand the language of the law.

When Allache, a young man from the Chemakum First Nation, stabbed Thomas Brown in Victoria on July 16, 1860, for Brown's assault on his wife, Allache was tried without legal counsel, but was provided with an interpreter—who did not speak his dialect. He became the first victim of judicial hanging in British Columbia. On the day prior to his trial the same court handed a white settler a four-year sentence for a similar crime. In a tragic postscript, *The British Colonist*, a leading newspaper, reported in November 1861 that Allache "was a much abused victim who should not have suffered death at all." "We hope we shall not have a repeat of that affair," said the editor. "If a man does not deserve to die, for the sake of humanity and the credit of justice, let the true facts be ascertained before it is too late."

Upper Canada (Ontario) was equally lucrative ground for the employment of executioners and holds the dubious distinction of hanging more men and women than any other jurisdiction in British North America, including the hanging of a 16-year-old girl for petty theft. John Sullivan of York paid with his life on October 11, 1798, for the forgery of a bank note worth less than $10. In Sandwich, Ontario, in 1828, a court sentenced Patrick Fitzgerald, a resident of Detroit, to hang for the rape and murder of the innkeeper's daughter. The hanging, a few days later, on the village common, drew over 3,000 spectators, many of whom camped out overnight to claim a front-row view. Three years later another man, Maurice Sellars, confessed on his deathbed that he, not Fitzgerald, had committed the crime.

Not to be outdone, authorities in Quebec made liberal use of the extreme penalty and, for good measure, combined hanging with additional medieval tortures to exact as much vengeance as possible. Thus David Maclean, an American citizen, when convicted of high treason in 1797 for inciting Quebecois to join the United States, was sentenced to be hanged—but not to the death: he was to be taken down while still alive and his bowels taken out and burned before his eyes. Then there was the curious case of Noel Francois, who aided and abetted his own demise when he was convicted of murder in 1825. He declared his innocence but argued at trial that he should be hanged anyway as punishment for his past crimes.

On the east coast, authorities pursued criminals with equal vigour and visited retribution on the guilty at every opportunity. In 1795 no fewer than 12 thieves were publicly hanged in Halifax, one for stealing potatoes from a farmer's field. Equally harsh were the courts in New Brunswick, where, in 1824, 18-year-old Patrick Bergen received the death penalty for the theft of 24 cents.

The law was no less severe in the colony of Newfoundland. In September 1750 William Gilmore was executed in St. John's for the theft of a cow. Eighty-five years later, in 1835, John Flood robbed the St. John's-Portugal Cove stagecoach and paid with his life in front of a large crowd outside the Duckworth Street courthouse, the last public hanging in Newfoundland.

Over a period of several hundred years, the gatekeepers of the justice system learned that a successful execution required a skilled hangman. It was a brutal trade and very few men could be found anywhere with the stomach to kill another at the end of a rope—so few, in fact, that on occasion, as was the case for Allache in 1860, the sheriff refused to conduct the gruesome task. A fellow inmate was recruited for the job, with the promise of a pardon and $50 for volunteering his services.

Those men who did come forward soon found themselves in great demand and earned respectable fees. John Robert Radclive, an apprentice of William Marwood, Britain's official hangman, came to Canada in 1890. He quickly earned a reputation for efficient executions from one side of the country to the other. By the time of his death in Toronto in 1912, he had officiated at the hangings of 132 men and women. His dedication to his craft, however, came at a steep price. By 1910, abandoned by his family, and deeply troubled by the memories of his victims, he had descended into alcoholism. In a final interview he stated, "they taunt me and haunt me until I am nearly crazy with an unearthly fear. I am two hundred times a murderer and I won't kill another man."

A similar fate awaited Arthur Bartholomew English (alias Arthur Ellis), who succeeded Radclive as Canada's unofficial hangman. He appeared on the scene in 1913 and, in a career that spanned over 20 years, performed more than 400 executions. He too fell victim to alcoholism. Shunned by his family, he died alone and in poverty at a squalid rooming house in Montreal in 1938.

Ellis was replaced by two other hangmen: a mysterious individual from Ontario using the trade name "Ellis," who could only be contacted through the sheriff of York county; and "Camille" Branchaud, who was retained by the Quebec government as its official hangman and made available to other jurisdictions outside the province. Most certainly one of these paid a less-than-friendly visit to St. John's, Newfoundland.

Two

Dearest dear and love divine
My heart is yours and yours is mine …

—Herb Spratt, love note
to Josephine O'Brien, 1941

James and Annie Spratt welcomed their youngest child into the world in June 1921. They christened him Herbert Augustus and he quickly became the centre of attention in a family that had grown steadily since their first child, Mollie, was born in 1905.

With Herb, James and Annie celebrated the arrival of their ninth child into their busy household on Pennywell Road, St. John's. Over the next six years, however, tragedy struck the Spratt family. In July 1924 their son Dermott and daughter Isabel died within days of each other during an outbreak of scarlet fever. In 1927, tuberculosis claimed the life of 17-year-old William.

The Spratts were well known in St. John's. Annie, a gentle and caring mother, ran the busy household and doted on her youngest son. James had married her in 1904. By then he had already built a reputation as an enterprising individual, first as a bookkeeper straight out of St. Patrick's Hall school, then, after an apprenticeship, as a skilled masonry tradesman. In 1907 he took the next step and formed his own small construction company. *McAlpine's Business Directory* for 1913 listed him as "James J. Spratt—Mason and Contractor."

The construction firm served the family well. By 1935, after 30 years in the building trades, Spratt decided he could comfortably retire and focus on his other interests, which included organized labour and local politics. He had never forgotten his working-class roots, and remained active in the union movement even as he ran his own small business. For nearly 40 years he remained secretary of the Bricklayers and Masons

Union in St. John's.

Spratt ran for one of six seats on city council in the municipal election of 1933 and was elected by a comfortable margin to an administration headed by Mayor Andrew Carnell. After the fateful decision by the Newfoundland government in November 1933 to abandon democracy and revert to colonial status, St. John's city council remained the only freely elected body on the island.

In the early years of World War II as the city government struggled with the additional demands placed on its services by the allied forces, Councillor Spratt spearheaded efforts to find additional sources of revenue through a city registration of vehicles and a surtax on gasoline. His efforts brought him into direct confrontation with powerful figures in the Commission of Government.

Spratt was re-elected in 1937 and in 1941. He was outspoken and energetic, with a direct approach to problem solving. If a city worker complained of unfair treatment, he raised the issue in council. If a city resident complained of poor sanitation services, Spratt took it upon himself to do an on-site inspection. His attention to detail earned him the respect of his colleagues and the voters of the city. Spratt took great satisfaction in his work.

Nineteen-year-old Herb Spratt enlisted in the Royal Navy in November 1940 as part of the 30th Overseas Contingent. Like hundreds of young men from the towns and villages of the crown colony, he volunteered to fight for his king and country.

James and Annie Spratt encouraged Herb's decision as a way for him to erase the shame of a six-month prison sentence he received a year earlier. As a teenage prank Herb and a young friend had used a toy gun to hold up grocer J.K. Bursell in Topsail, just outside of St. John's, on the evening of October 10, 1939. The rattled storekeeper handed over $20 in change and a cheque for $14. Bursell was able to identify the boys to police.

At sentencing on November 20, Chief Justice Horwood remarked on the senseless nature of the crime and wished he could send the boys to a reformatory. He found it regrettable that no such institution existed in the colony. "The unfortunate thing is the youths have done something which blights their future," said Horwood. He then sentenced the two to six months of hard labour in His Majesty's Penitentiary.

By the spring of 1940, with a few weeks off for good behaviour, the boys were released. Prison had focused Herb's mind, and he had decided where his future lay.

For a few weeks Herb performed well in basic training at the Royal Navy Base, Shotley, in Suffolk, England. But the cold and damp English autumn aggravated a severe respiratory problem soon diagnosed as pulmonary tuberculosis, probably contracted during his stay at the penitentiary. By early May 1941, after four months in a sanitorium, Herb's health began to improve; however, the Admiralty Board had already determined he would not fully recover in time to make an effective seaman. The Royal Navy gave him an honorable discharge on medical grounds and arranged for his return to Newfoundland on HMS *Rodney*, which was crossing the Atlantic for refit in North America.

Herb reported to the *Rodney*'s sick-bay petty officer on May 21, 1941. He handed the officer his discharge papers from the Admiralty Board. A medical attendant led the frail young man below deck to his hospital bed in the ship's infirmary to await its departure for Halifax and repatriation to St. John's, Newfoundland.

The *Rodney*, one of the most powerful battle cruisers in the British fleet, left its base at Greenock on the west coast of Scotland in the late evening hours of May 22, providing heavy escort for a convoy crossing the North Atlantic to Halifax. On board were several hundred officers and seamen from the United States, Canada, and Newfoundland. Some were on leave, while others, like Herb, were seriously ill and confined to the ship's infirmary.

Seas were calm, and under a crescent moon the convoy moved at a steady speed down the Firth of Clyde and out into the North Atlantic. After setting a course for Halifax the crew settled in for what they hoped would be an uneventful crossing.

On the night of May 24, the *Rodney* received a signal that HMS *Hood* had sunk after being hit by a shell from the German battleship *Bismarck*. Over 1,400 men were lost. On orders from the Admiralty, the *Rodney*'s skipper, Captain Dalrymple-Hamilton, veered his ship about, left the convoy, and gave chase to the *Bismarck*.

Dalrymple-Hamilton informed his ship's company of the change in plans and turned his thoughts to intercepting the enemy ship. The *Bis-*

marck was now attempting to evade the British Navy and reach the safety of its base in occupied France. After a day of worsening weather and conflicting reports on the whereabouts of their quarry, RAF Swordfish planes spotted the *Bismarck* and successfully hit its rudder with one of their torpedoes.

With a disabled and jammed steering column, the German ship could only manoeuvre to port in ever-widening circles. The *Rodney* spotted its crippled prey at 8:45 a.m. on May 27 and the battle that ensued raged in the teeth of a force eight gale.

As Herb lay helplessly in the sick bay, the thunder of the *Rodney*'s massive 16-inch guns reverberated through the ship. Within an hour, the *Bismarck*, unable to counter the shell fire, was in flames, and the British warship closed to a few thousand yards: point-blank range.

Normally the long gun barrels were elevated for a range of 10,000 yards, but now with the two ships at close quarters the barrels were lowered to such a degree that powerful blast waves shook the deck plates and rolled through the bowels of the ship. As each gun fired, the concussion throughout the *Rodney* shattered ceramic toilets and urinals, popped rivets from partitions, and ruptured water pipes on the lower decks.

Coupled with the thunder of the guns, the ship rolled and pitched in the 50-knot northwesterly gale and massive waves broke over the bow. Crew quarters were destroyed and those in the sick bay were lashed down to prevent being tossed around and striking the guard rails around the beds. An unknown sailor later recorded the chaotic scene in his diary: "Meanwhile on board *Rodney* the crew were having a bad time. The sickbay was wrecked. The chief's and petty officers' flat was wrecked … All the electrical systems on board were out of order. And the water was coming in through the hatches."

By 10:45 a.m., running critically low on fuel and ammunition, the *Rodney* broke off the action on orders from the flagship, *King George V*, just as the *Bismarck* was slipping beneath the waves. The *Rodney* had fired nearly 400 high explosive shells from her big guns, most of which had found their mark. Under constant attack from German aircraft and still in heavy seas, the *Rodney* returned to home base at Greenock for emergency repairs and refueling before attempting a second Atlantic crossing to Halifax.

Preparations for the crossing took another three days. After departing on May 31, HMS *Rodney* arrived in Halifax on June 6, 1941, to discharge those in the sick bay before continuing to Boston for a major refit. Herb Spratt began his journey back to St. John's the next day.

Despite his bitter disappointment at having been discharged from the Royal Navy, Herb began to look to the future. He was relatively well educated. After finishing Grade 10 at St. Bonaventure's College before the war, he had enrolled in a commercial course delivered by Mercy Convent and had become proficient in typing, shorthand, and bookkeeping. With these skills and his Navy record he secured a good job at the end of August as a checker with the Cape Construction Company across the street from his brother's home on Plymouth Road in St. John's. The job paid well and he had money in his pocket.

Herb also renewed his friendship with Josephine O'Brien, an attractive young woman from Cape Broyle whom he had met in the summer of 1940. She had come to the city to work as a servant girl for a family on Pennywell Road. Josephine had stayed with that family for only a few months before moving to the Chesman household on Hill O'Chips.

St. John's in 1941 hummed with the activity of war but the city offered the young woman none of the easy friendliness of her Southern Shore community nor the support of her close-knit family. Josephine, born in 1921 to William and Bridget O'Brien, was the ninth child in a still-growing household. Two more children followed her birth. William and Bridget were hardworking parents devoted to their children even as, one by one, they left home to begin lives of their own.

Josephine found it tough to adjust to city life. Although Cape Broyle was barely 40 miles south of St. John's, the rough gravel road and the demands of her job meant isolation from her family. She battled loneliness and only occasionally could she keep company with her older sister, Mary, who worked at Modern Clothing on Water Street.

Quite naturally Josephine fell for the devoted attention and lavish gifts from Herb. Every day he came home from work, donned his best suit and overcoat, and walked to Hill O'Chips to pick up his girl. They window-shopped, walked in Bannerman Park, and sometimes treated themselves to the latest Hollywood film at one of the many theatres in town.

The relationship blossomed. Herb and Josephine were very much in love by the fall of 1941. In the fashion of the time, Herb composed love notes to Josephine and slipped them to her along with the gifts as proof of his undying love. The two began to make lifelong plans.

Sometime in the early fall of 1941, before the winter storms closed the gravel road, Josephine invited Herb to meet her father and mother in Cape Broyle, an indication that the relationship might lead to marriage. Herb borrowed his father's car for the occasion. The day trip appeared to go smoothly, but William O'Brien's introduction to his daughter's boyfriend left him with a strong sense of foreboding. "He was a bit strange. There was something wrong with him," he later told his family.

Josephine expressed her own worries about Herb. She confided to Mary that she was uneasy about his behaviour. At times he was extremely jealous and prone to outbursts of anger. For a while she stopped wearing Herb's ring and seriously considered breaking off the relationship.

But Josephine mentioned none of these misgivings in a letter to her father dated March 2, 1942. For his birthday, March 4, she promised to send him tobacco or a $2 bill if she couldn't find a way to get him the tobacco. "I would love to be able to send more," she said, "but all the money in the world could not pay you for all you have done for us." In a light touch she asked her father to reveal his age: "Every year I ask the same question, but I am no wiser than when I first asked it."

Josephine's sense of humour came through even in her postscript. "How is mom, busy praying, I guess, and good enough to last ye for a while. How is Rita, Bern, John, and Char?" She concluded her letter by enquiring after the family pet, "poor old Topsy."

Everyone in Herb's family was delighted with Josephine. They assumed that the couple would be married in the near future. Confirmation came in late October when a notice of their engagement and a June wedding announcement appeared in the papers. No one knew who placed the announcement; the family simply assumed it was Herb's father, eager to let the world know that his youngest son was finally settling down.

Tuesday, March 17, 1942, dawned clear and cold in St. John's. Despite the chill and the somber war news, St. Patrick's Day, a public holiday in the colony, ignited passionate celebrations everywhere in Newfoundland among both Catholics and Protestants. The city, with its strong

Irish-Catholic roots, took a well-earned respite from the tensions of unending conflict.

Every day, it seemed, damaged merchant ships limped through the Narrows of St. John's Harbour with their wounded and their dead, casualties from running the deadly gauntlet with German submarines while crossing the North Atlantic. The anti-aircraft batteries on Hill O'Chips and the Southside Hills reinforced the ever-present fear of enemy attack. In early 1942 the people of St. John's sat in their blacked-out homes at night and worried about what would happen next.

The *Daily News* and the *Evening Telegram* devoted their front pages to the fighting: "Daylight raids by the RAF on Germany; 240,000 Jews slain by the Nazis in Ukraine; US smashes Jap invasion fleet off New Guinea." Stories of carnage and disaster dominated on the BBC Overseas Service and on WEAF, the local American Forces station at Fort Pepperrell.

In St. John's and throughout Newfoundland the new prosperity of war tempered the bitter memories of the depression years. Canadians, Americans, and the British poured money into the construction of bases in strategic locations such as Gander, Botwood, and Torbay.

The Canadian forces arrived in 1940 and erected large military camps on the slopes of the Southside Hills and at Lester's Field near Mundy Pond. At the end of January 1941 the massive troopship *Edmund B. Alexander* docked at the eastern end of the harbour and 1,000 American soldiers disembarked to man installations around the city. The Yanks had arrived in force and the US Army Corps of Engineers soon issued a call for 500 labourers to work in the construction of Fort Pepperrell. A basic wage of 40 cents an hour was promised and job levels were expected to expand for the next several years.

Around the Avalon Peninsula young men and women deserted the hardscrabble life of the outports and the unpredictable fishery for wage employment in construction and service jobs in the city. Energetic men with some schooling were needed as timekeepers and labourers on the Canadian bases. Young ladies were needed as cash assistants at the London, New York and Paris on Water Street. Male assistants were needed at Steers. In a city short on housing, landlords recognized opportunity and scrambled to convert every available space into rental properties.

The resident population of St. John's had grown to 40,000 by 1942 and was largely hemmed into the space between Water Street and Empire

Avenue. Beyond, toward Mt. Scio, sheep and cattle grazed in open fields and small farms produced food for markets in the city.

From January 1941 to January 1942, the total number of individuals on able-bodied relief in the colony dropped from 39,000 to just over 8,000 and costs to the government declined from $80,000 to $26,000 for the whole of the island and Labrador.

The establishment of regular airline flights by Trans Canada Airlines between cities in Canada and points in Newfoundland was further indication that the wartime economy was booming. The Newfoundland Railway announced additional express runs to its schedule to accommodate the new demands across the island.

The influx of some 15,000 servicemen from Canada and the US and the prosperity brought by the all-out war effort resulted in a dynamic social scene in St. John's. No less than five movie theatres featured the latest Hollywood productions. *International Squadron*, starring Ronald Reagan, played at the Nickel, while at the Capitol one of the year's best films, *The Feminine Touch*, an MGM comedy starring Rosalind Russell, drew large crowds. Money, danger, and romance fueled the excitement of the city.

Prosperity also brought its challenges. St. John's city council wrestled with providing basic services to the military installations. Immediately after the election in December 1941, a special committee of council headed by Councillor Spratt took on the issue of snow clearing and disposal—always a problem in St. John's, even in peacetime, but with increased wartime construction these services were strained to the breaking point in the winter of 1941/42. In a pointed letter to Edward Emerson, Commissioner of Justice and Defence, in January 1942, Spratt warned that the city could not voluntarily assume any additional burdens because of defence necessities. He reminded the commissioner that the burden of these extra services was a responsibility of the Commission of Government for Newfoundland.

The Newfoundland Constabulary—the city's police force—struggled to cope with the reality of wartime St. John's. The American and Canadian forces brought with them a dramatic increase in the number of military vehicles on city streets. Officers with whistles directed the traffic flow at busy intersections and a short while later the first traffic lights in

St. John's were installed at Rawlins Cross, which had become a bottleneck into the downtown area.

Petty crime was on the rise; the magistrate's court dealt with lengthy dockets every week. On Monday, March 16, 1942, Magistrate Browne imposed a $100 fine on a female resident of New Gower Street for trafficking in liquor. He then levied an additional $10 penalty for her threats to throw boiling water over a police officer; a laundry steward received a six-month jail sentence for the theft of cigarettes and antifreeze at the United Services Organization (USO) club; a Canadian sailor refused to take his proper place in a lineup at the Nickel Theatre and received a $2 fine for his rude behaviour; and the driver of a horse and cart received a $20 fine for being impaired while operating a moving vehicle.

While the Constabulary managed rowdiness and public drunkenness, other alarming cases pointed to the new stresses and strains of life in the city. On March 12, a young woman from Bell Island tried to end her life by jumping into the waters of Baird's Cove. After being rescued by two police officers she was charged with attempted suicide, a criminal offence. Browne remanded the woman to eight days in jail pending a full review of her case.

In the downtown area, unaccompanied females found themselves the targets of aggressive behaviour from the many merchant seamen in port. Two such sailors, arrested for public harassment of a young woman outside the Star Theatre on March 14, received a stern lecture from Browne. He then sentenced both men to a month's imprisonment.

Most city residents considered any turmoil in their daily lives a small price to pay in the struggle to defeat the enemy. Nevertheless, they welcomed any opportunity to party and to forget, at least temporarily, about the battle that was moving ever closer to their shores.

The 1942 St. Patrick's Day celebrations featured numerous events starring local performers, the centrepiece being the annual gala organized by the Benevolent Irish Society (BIS). At Government House the BIS officers were received in the afternoon by the ever-gracious Lady Walwyn and His Excellency, Sir Humphrey Walwyn, resplendent in his naval uniform. On behalf of the king, and the Commission of Government for Newfoundland, Walwyn commended the organization for its expressions of loyalty to the crown.

The festivities began early. A late frolic on St. Patrick's eve started at the Majestic after midnight and continued into the wee hours. Lafosse and his Orchestra, with help from some talented British sailors, charmed the partygoers. Afternoon and evening performances of *Spring Time in Erin*, an Irish comedy presented by the St. Patrick's Hall players at Pitts Memorial Hall on Long's Hill, had sold out a week earlier. Latecomers bought standing-room-only tickets.

The Rhythm Kings highlighted the show at the Old Colony Club, where Canadian and American military officers purchased most of the tickets for the crowded dance night. At St. Patrick's Hall auditorium on Deanery Avenue and Convent Square, Miss Kitty Picott thrilled the audience with her renditions of "When Irish Eyes Are Smiling" and "In the Garden of Tomorrow." Concertgoers faced long lineups for the matinee and evening concerts outside the entrance to the auditorium.

Herb Spratt came home from work at 1 p.m. on St. Patrick's Day to spend the afternoon with Josephine. They had arranged the previous night to meet around 3 p.m. at his brother Edward's home at 33 Plymouth Road in the east end of St. John's. It was only a short walk from the Chesman house on Hill O'Chips where Josephine worked.

Edward, his wife, Maud, and their two young daughters occupied the small ground-floor flat at 33 Plymouth. As with most modest flats in St. John's, the kitchen doubled as a living room with a comfortable couch placed next to the window overlooking the east end of Duckworth Street. The curtains were closed at night to maintain privacy and to meet the requirements of the wartime blackout. Above the kitchen was the bedroom of Ambrose and Beatrice Lynch, who owned the building and occupied the upstairs flat along with their five boarders and a servant girl.

Herb and Josephine spent just about every spare moment at Edward and Maud's flat on Plymouth Road. Most nights the four of them sat around the kitchen table chatting and playing cards. At other times they cared for the two little girls when Edward and Maud were out. Maud was particularly struck by the couple's happiness. As she later testified, Herb and Josephine "were very fond of each other, always gay and carrying on."

Maud had already left with the two children to spend the evening with her sister on Job Street when Herb and Josephine arrived at the flat around 4:30 p.m. Edward sensed that something big was in the air when his brother, looking dapper in his blue serge suit and matching quiff hat, strolled in the door with Josephine on his arm.

Josephine removed her coat and white silk scarf before taking a chair by the stove, proudly showing off her engagement ring and the new wristwatch Herb had given her for Christmas. Herb sat contentedly at the kitchen table quietly smoking a cigarette, deep in thought. "Well, we're definitely getting married. It's going to be a June wedding ... June 14," he declared proudly after a few minutes of silence.

"June's the best month to get married ... it brings good luck," said Josephine. "Ed, we want you to stand for us, be our best man ..."

Herb interrupted angrily. "Someone put it in the papers," he shouted, "so it's no longer a secret." Edward was startled by the sudden outburst. After an uncomfortable silence, Herb calmed down and began talking of his worries about finding a place to live when they were married.

The young couple left about 4:45 p.m. to go for a walk uptown, along Duckworth, to look at the movie posters and then down to busy Water Street, where most stores were preparing to close for the day. Before long the chill of a brisk northwest wind biting into their faces forced them to go back to Plymouth Road. Herb went into the cornerstore next door to buy ice cream.

Edward had already left when they arrived home. The coal fire had died in the small stove and the kitchen was cool. Herb and Josephine sat at the table enjoying the ice cream and discussed whether they would go to see *The Feminine Touch* at the Capitol Theatre. Josephine complained of a headache and, in the end, Herb decided the long lineup wasn't worth it. They decided to stay put until Edward and Maud returned.

Herb later recalled some of what happened next. He claimed that he and Josephine had been lying on the couch talking and kissing like any young couple would. Out of the blue, Josephine told him she was going to have a baby. (A police reconstruction of the scene revealed Herb's violent reaction to Josephine's words.)

Without warning, Herb's fist smashed into Josephine's face. The force of the blow broke off her front tooth and left her in shock. Semi-conscious, she slumped against the armrest at the end of the couch, weakly trying to shield her head with her arm. Herb grabbed an electric iron from the stovetop and, with the pointed end, struck again and again with lethal force. Finally, with a slight moan, Josephine succumbed.

Herb knew it was all over. His clothing and hands covered with blood, he dropped the iron, grabbed his overcoat, and stumbled out into the night.

Just after 11:15 p.m. Maud Spratt opened the door of her Plymouth Road flat and switched on the light in the kitchen. For a moment she stood rooted to the spot, suspended in disbelief. She nearly dropped the child she held in her arms. Then the awful reality dawned: the girl slumped on the couch was dead.

Edward, who had been outside paying the taxi driver, was just coming in the door when he heard his wife's screams. Maud ran down the hallway toward him, her face deathly pale. He rushed past her into the kitchen, not knowing what to expect. There, he saw the body of Josephine O'Brien sprawled, half-sitting, half-lying, on the couch, her face covered in blood and her head thrown back at an odd angle. A bloody iron lay next to her. Edward rushed back into the hallway and phoned the police.

Sergeant Manderson took the incoming call. A male voice on the other end of the line shouted, "Send a couple of police to 33 Plymouth Road, we are having a murder here." A woman screamed in the background. Constable Harold Brazil was immediately dispatched to the scene. Because no police van was available, he walked along Duckworth as far as the War Memorial, where he met up with Constables Barrett and Tucker. All three hurried to Plymouth Road.

Suspecting the worst, Edward had phoned his parents' home on Pennywell Road. His mother and father, along with his brother Gerard arrived a few minutes ahead of the police. When the three constables reached 33 Plymouth Road around 11:40 p.m., Mr. and Mrs. Spratt were standing outside. Edward and Gerard Spratt met the officers at the door and directed them to the kitchen.

Brazil secured the crime scene, ordering everyone, including those who lived upstairs, to remain inside. Constable Tucker phoned the chief of police, who dispatched Sergeant William Case of the Criminal Investigation Division (CID) and the government pathologist, Dr. Joseph Josephson, to the crime scene.

Interviews with Mr. and Mrs. Lynch and their five boarders produced no solid leads. The boarders had come and gone as usual from 4 p.m. to 11:30 p.m. without noticing or hearing anything unusual. Mrs. Lynch had been to her bedroom directly above the kitchen several times that evening but had not heard a sound out of the ordinary.

In his seven years as a detective with the CID, Case had never witnessed a more gruesome scene. At the magisterial inquiry he described what he had seen when he walked into the Spratt kitchen on the night of March 17:

> On the couch I noticed the body of a girl in a reclining position, the left shoulder and head resting on the head of the couch, the legs extending to the floor. The head was covered with blood and on the right side in the region of the temple and the ear I noticed a large wound, but there was such a quantity of dried blood around the head that it was impossible to ascertain the other injuries at the time. The right hand was partly clenched. I felt the hand and forearm; the flesh was icy cold …

After interviewing Edward and Gerard Spratt, Case sent out a call for the arrest of Herb Spratt.

Herb's brother Ray, who lived at 144 Water Street, had decided to stay home on St. Patrick's night while his wife, Theresa, and her mother went off to the concert at St. Patrick's auditorium. At 10:45 p.m. he went into the hall and switched on the light to put more coal in the stove. At that moment Herb came in the door. Ray thought at first that his brother was drunk, as Herb came over and put his arms around him, saying, "You are the best brother I got. I love you."

Ray led his brother into the kitchen and had him lie down on the couch. Herb was agitated and raving. "I killed my girl," he said, sobbing. "She was going to have a baby. I never had anything to do with a girl in my life."

Despite Herb's uncharacteristic behaviour, Ray could not smell alcohol and he had never known his brother to drink. Herb pulled himself together somewhat and asked his brother for 10 cents to buy a beer, handing over his empty wallet to Ray at the same time.

"I had $35 in my wallet," said Herb. "I don't know if I spent it or if someone stole it from me."

Becoming more and more alarmed, Ray told his brother to stay put while he ran next door to phone his father. Ray rushed back a few minutes later only to find that Herb had left.

Hubert Murphy, a first cousin of the Spratts, lived on Alexander Street. He also thought Herb had been drinking when he showed up at the door sometime after 11 p.m. "He came into the kitchen, flopped down on a chair by the head of the couch, and didn't say anything for a while. He looked very drunk and started rambling on about having killed his girlfriend," said Hubert. "His eyes were bloodshot but there was not the least smell of alcohol. Then he told me he'd killed her by hitting her with his fist and then with an iron. He'd taken her down a box of chocolates and she told him she was going to have a baby. 'I suppose she's dead by now ... I guess I'll be hung tomorrow,' he told me. He asked me for ten cents and I gave it to him just to get clear of him. He left and I saw him cross the street."

Hubert's younger brother, Terrence, had performed in the concert at St. Patrick's auditorium and didn't get home until 11:30 p.m. He went looking for Herb as soon as Hubert told him what had happened. Unable to find him downtown or at his home on Pennywell Road, Terrence hurried back to Water Street. When he walked into Ray's home at 12:30 a.m., he found Herb lying down across two chairs in the front room with his hat and coat on.

"At first I thought he was drunk," explained Terrence, "then he seemed delirious. I took off his hat and gloves and loosened his collar and told him to go to sleep. He was crying and praying and asking God what he should do."

Herb seemed unaware of others in the room and continued talking to himself about Josephine and asking God why He had let him do it. He turned to Terrence. "You don't believe me, do you?" He pulled open his jacket to show his blood-spattered shirt.

Theresa was trying to get the baby asleep upstairs amidst the commotion and noise downstairs in the front room. When she heard Terrence come in, she pulled on her dress, took the baby in her arms, and hurried downstairs. She asked Herb what was wrong.

"I did something awful," he moaned. "I killed my girl and I want some place to stay for the night."

Theresa led Herb to the kitchen and told him to lie down on the couch. He started to cry.

"I bought a locket for her for Easter and paid $8.50 for it but I didn't give it to her yet." He sobbed. "I love that girl. She said she was going to have a baby and I hit her and I killed her."

There was a pause and Herb continued, "I don't know if I killed her yesterday or six o'clock or the day before or the day before. What did I do it for?"

Theresa went back upstairs to try and get the baby asleep but Herb was shouting and Terrence was telling him to knock it off and be quiet. After the baby finally fell asleep around 1:30 a.m., she went downstairs again just as Constable Harold March and another officer came in the front door.

Herb was still sobbing uncontrollably when he was taken from the van into the police station on Duckworth Street. Case returned to the station at 1:45 a.m. Herb was sitting between Constables Healey and Davis. Case recognized him as the same person he had arrested in 1939 for the robbery in Topsail. At that time he had sternly counselled Herb and had done his best to have the charges of robbery and being armed with an offensive weapon—charges which could have resulted in a five-year sentence—reduced to a lesser charge of robbery with aggravation.

Case spoke to Herb and called him by name. "He had just stopped crying," observed Case, "the eyes were swollen and he was suffering from emotion. I studied him for a minute or two to see if there was any sign of intoxication but could not find any."

Herb also recognized Case. "You were a friend to me before, Sergeant," said Herb. "I want you to be a friend to me now."

But this situation was far more serious than Herb's previous arrest. Case informed Herb that he was a suspect in the murder of Josephine O'Brien at 33 Plymouth Road. He read him his rights and after about five minutes took him into an office.

Case recorded verbatim the rambling statement which Herb seemed eager to provide. Without any prompting, Herb recalled the several hours before the attack when he and Josephine had strolled hand in hand down Water Street and later when they returned to his brother Edward's flat on Plymouth Road. He remembered striking her with his fist and just once with the iron. He remembered Josephine's groan, then seeing blood on her face. What happened after that was a blank. He repeated, "Why did

I do it? I loved her." Herb had made no effort to remove the bloodstains from his clothing and his hands.

On Wednesday, March 18, Herb was arraigned before Browne in Magistrate's Court in St. John's and formally charged with the murder of Josephine O'Brien. A journalist for the *Evening Telegram* reported from the courthouse: "As the charge was being read the accused showed considerable emotion and fell across the bar. The constables had to assist him to a chair until the proceedings terminated when he was taken downstairs and locked up on remand for eight days."

The police began the process of reconstructing the chain of events that led to the murder and taking statements from witnesses.

Josephine's body was removed to the city morgue in the early morning hours of March 18.

Knowing that they would be called as witnesses in court, Dr. Thomas Anderson, chief coroner, and Dr. Josephson, the government pathologist, recorded precise details as they performed a post-mortem on the body. Anderson noted that

> She was a well-developed girl about twenty years of age, five feet two inches in height and weighing about 125 lbs. Her face was disfigured with clotted blood, her lip was bruised and one tooth was broken off. There were three large wounds in the region of the eye extending towards the ear. The ear attachments had been separated from the skull and there was a large wound behind the ear in which there were brain tissue and bone fragments. One of the fingernails was torn off. There were eight distinct wounds of penetration on the body and these could have been inflicted with the sharp edge of a flat iron. The injury to the victim's mouth was due to a fist blow and likely happened before death. Internal examination showed the internal organs were normal and healthy. There was absolutely no evidence of pregnancy. Death was due to skull fractures, haemorrhage and shock.

After the autopsy, Josephine's body was prepared for burial at Caul's Funeral Parlour. On Thursday, March 19, Josephine's brother Johnny arrived in his pickup to bring his sister's body home to Cape Broyle. On instructions from the Newfoundland Constabulary, the casket was to remain closed.

The preliminary inquiry into the death of Josephine O'Brien convened in St. John's on March 30 with Magistrate Hugh O'Neill presiding. The prisoner did not have legal counsel. A total of 20 witnesses, including Herb's brothers Ray and Edward, as well as their wives, Theresa and Maud, gave evidence over a period of five days. The result was a foregone conclusion and on April 4 an indictment was handed down by the court. The charge was read to the prisoner: "that the said accused at St. John's, on the seventeenth day of March, 1942 … murdered one Josephine O'Brien, against the Peace of our Lord the King, his Crown and Dignity." The next act of the tragedy would be staged in the Supreme Court of Newfoundland.

Three

Show no pity for life, eye for eye, tooth for tooth ...
—Deuteronomy 19:21

Monday, April 27, dawned sunny and mild in St. John's. Temperatures had hovered just above the zero mark for several days. People were more than ready to bid winter goodbye. Around the spacious grounds of Government House and in Bannerman Park colourful crocuses were blooming. Downtown, along the narrow streets, residents coped with the inevitable clouds of dust as employees of the city's sanitary department collected loads of ashes and garbage in their open horse-drawn carts.

A minor outbreak of diphtheria worried parents in the city as did warnings about cases of measles and scarlet fever. Grave war news continued to dominate the airwaves and, predictably, each day the press carried a new list of local boys who had become casualties.

Few people noticed the black prison van transporting Herb Spratt from His Majesty's Penitentiary on Forest Road to the Newfoundland Supreme Court Building on Water Street, where, manacled, he was led up the steps into the building by two Constabulary officers.

Spratt had been on suicide watch since his arrival at the prison on March 18. He suffered daily fits of hysteria and violent trembling, followed by exhaustion and profuse sweating. Superintendent Byrne ordered around-the-clock observation as Spratt's mental health deteriorated. The prison doctor prescribed sedatives to treat severe headaches. On numerous occasions wardens entered the cell to restrain him as he banged his head repeatedly on his cell walls.

The crown's case against Spratt for the wilful murder of Josephine O'Brien began at 10 a.m. on April 27 in front of Chief Justice Horwood.

Horwood had been in his position so long that no one in the courtroom that day would have remembered anyone else in the chief justice's chair. His birth in colonial St. John's on November 5, 1862, during the reign of Queen Victoria, came nearly six years before Upper and Lower Canada, along with Nova Scotia, New Brunswick, and Prince Edward Island, agreed to form a new country called Canada. Horwood attended Bishop Feild College, studied law, and was admitted to the Newfoundland bar in 1885. He entered politics in 1894 and was elected three times to the legislative assembly.

In his short but notable political career Horwood had been appointed to the commission negotiating the terms of confederation with Canada in 1895. Later he became the minister without portfolio in Prime Minister Whiteway's administration from 1895 to 1897 and attorney general with the Sir Robert Bond government from 1900 to 1902. On July 31, 1902, he accepted an appointment as chief justice of the Supreme Court. At the age of 80, he was steeped in the English legal system, which had changed very little in the previous half century.

Heading the prosecution was another veteran of the Newfoundland justice system, Lewis Edward Emerson. Edward, born to George and Katherine Emerson, a prominent St. John's family, in 1890, received his primary education at St. Patrick's Hall in St. John's and displayed early academic promise. As was the case for most sons of the upper class in the city, his father sent him to one of the best boarding schools in England. Edward entered the prestigious Catholic boys' school, Ampleforth College, set in the rolling hills of north Yorkshire.

As Edward's father practised law and became a Supreme Court justice, it was not surprising that Edward was predisposed to the legal profession. On April 12, 1913, at age 23, Emerson was admitted to the Newfoundland bar. During his early career as a practising lawyer, he attained a measure of fame in legal circles for his spirited defence of Wo Fen Game, who was charged in 1922 with the murder of three of his co-workers at the Chinese laundry on Murray Street in St. John's. Although Wo Fen was convicted and sentenced to hang, Emerson's skills as a criminal lawyer were on prominent display throughout the trial.

Like many in his profession at the time, Emerson took the natural step from the courtroom to politics. In 1924 he was appointed by Prime Minister Hickman as minister without portfolio, but in the June general election he lost in the district of St. John's East and resigned from Cabinet. Undeterred, he ran successfully for the district of Placentia East in 1928. In 1932 he returned to the district of St. John's East and was re-elected to the Newfoundland Assembly. Prime Minister Alderdice, who came to power in 1932, appointed Emerson as his minister of justice and attorney general. The appointment ended abruptly in February 1934, with the termination of democratic rule in Newfoundland and the appointment by Britain of a governor and six commissioners to manage the colony.

When the Dominions Office in London asked Governor Anderson to recommend Newfoundlanders who might be suitable commissioners in the new colonial government, Emerson should have been a logical choice. But, in Anderson's words, Emerson was "bumptious ... and there are doubts about his strict honesty"—opinions which were not far off the mark in light of later events.

Despite his career setback, Emerson remained a fixture among the social elite in the city. On weekends and holidays he spent much of his time at the exclusive Bally Haly Golf Club or pursuing his other interests, driving the gravel highways of the Avalon and fishing the salmon rivers. His St. John's residence was located in the upscale district on Circular Road but the family gravitated to their comfortable residence at Virginia Lake on Logy Bay Road during the summers.

In a short sojourn from politics, Emerson returned to private practice and in 1935 entered a partnership with J.P. Blackwood and Eric Cook. He remained in the public eye, however, and two years later the Dominions Office overcame its earlier misgivings and appointed him attorney general and Commissioner of Justice. In addition to his complex duties as commissioner, his role as attorney general required him to act as chief crown prosecutor in serious criminal cases.

Assisting Emerson in the prosecution of Spratt was the director of public prosecutions, Henry Pyne Carter, also a skilled lawyer. He graduated from Bishop's College in Lennoxville, Quebec, and practised law in London, England, before returning to Newfoundland in 1926 to enter private practice in St. John's. He joined the attorney general's department in 1934.

James A. Power took on the formidable task of defending Spratt. An alumnus of St. Bonaventure's College, he was called to the Newfoundland bar in 1926 and started his own law practice out of the Kearney Building in St. John's. Power came to this trial with no experience in serious criminal cases. He faced an unequal struggle against an overwhelming array of privilege, training, and experience.

Only a few spectators filled the gallery when the murder trial began at 10 a.m. on April 27. The press paid little attention in the lead-up to trial; the war remained foremost in the public mind. For most St. John's residents, the murder was old news, and justice would inevitably take its course. The court had already selected the 12-man jury and, with the appointment of P.R. McCormac as jury chair, all was in readiness.

Carter opened the case for the prosecution by outlining the known facts of the case: that the accused, Herbert Spratt, and the victim, Josephine O'Brien, had been keeping company for some time and their engagement had been announced in the paper; that on the night of March 17, Edward Spratt, brother of the accused, and his wife, Maud, returned to their flat at 33 Plymouth Road to find the blood-splattered body of the victim sprawled on their couch in the kitchen; that they had called the police; and that later on that night, the accused was arrested at the home of another brother, Raymond, who lived at 144 Water Street.

Eric St. George, a 10-year veteran of the CID, took the stand first. He described the layout of 33 Plymouth Road and placed a diagram of the ground floor in evidence. In response to prosecution questions he directed the jury's attention to the location of the kitchen, the location of the stairs to the flat above, the shared bathroom off the hallway on the first floor, and the kitchen window overlooking Duckworth Street. There was no cross-examination.

Constable Harold J. March, an expert in fingerprinting and photography, took the stand next. He had been called from his home on Cookstown Road at midnight on March 17 and had proceeded to Plymouth Road after picking up his equipment at the police station. He had taken numerous photographs of the crime scene and had removed the iron for fingerprinting. March indicated that he was then instructed by Case to proceed to 144 Water Street to pick up Spratt. Accompanying March in the police van were Constables Davis, Healey, Morrissey, and Lacey. March described their arrival and the subsequent arrest:

We arrived at five minutes to one. I opened the door and went in the hall followed by Constables Healey and Davis. I saw a woman on the stairs and I asked her if Herb Spratt was in. She said "yes, in the kitchen." I carried on into the kitchen and saw the accused lying on the couch, the accused here present.... I called Spratt by his surname, Spratt, and assisted him to a sitting position.... He was crying very hard—moaning, sobbing—and he appeared in a dazed condition. I told him he was wanted in connection with the death of a girl on Plymouth Road and he had to go with us. He did not pay any attention. He looked around the room and then lay down on the couch again crying louder than before. I picked him up again to a sitting position. Then the two constables came along who were with me. They picked him up between them and took him out to the police van. I walked out behind and got in the police van. He was still crying very hard and began to talk.... I cautioned him. I said "you are not bound to say anything. Anything you say may be used in evidence later ..." He did not pay any attention to me.

March described their arrival at CID headquarters around 1 a.m. Spratt was brought into the main office and seated at a table.

He was in a very bad way when we arrived and for some time afterwards ... laying his head on the table, crying and moaning. He began to talk about necklaces, a wrist watch and other articles. When I saw that he was going to talk, I again cautioned him. Sgt. Case arrived in about half an hour and charged him with the murder of Josephine O'Brien and cautioned him. After the caution Spratt said he wanted to make a statement. He said, "If she's dead, I want to die, too."

Emerson called Maud Spratt, the third witness of the day, to the stand. She described arriving home by taxi about 11:30 p.m. on March

17 with her husband, Edward, and their two young daughters. While Edward was paying for the taxi, she had gone in the unlocked front door and down the hallway, holding the youngest child while the older girl followed her. She opened the kitchen door and turned on the light switch just inside. Emerson then led the witness through the scene in front of her that night:

> Q. And when you turned on the switch you saw … perhaps you will describe what you saw.
> A. I saw the girl lying on the couch.
> Q. How did she appear?
> A. She was lying down on her side with her two hands down. I could not see her face.
> Q. Why?
> A. It was covered with blood, and her hair was down over her face.
> Q. Did you recognize the girl?
> A. Yes, I recognized her by her clothes.
> Q. Did you see anything else?
> A. The iron was laid on the couch beside her.

Under Power's cross-examination, Maud described an affectionate relationship between her brother-in-law and Josephine. A few days prior to the murder Herb had shown her an expensive necklace he had bought for Josephine for Easter. He and Josephine had been coming to Maud and Edward's flat just about every day for the past several months. Often they took care of the children when she was away. Power's questions focused on the pending marriage:

> Q. Had either of them ever told you about their marriage plans beyond the fact that they were to be married in June? Did either of them ever say anything to you about looking for a place to live?
> A. No, not to me.
> Q. Do you know if either of them said anything about purchasing furniture or making a payment for furniture?

A. I heard Herbert say that he was paying on bedroom furniture.

Q. Did he say where?

A. No.

Q. But you heard him say that he was paying; not that he was going to pay or anything like that; but he actually was.

A. Yes.

Edward's testimony supported his wife's version of the events. He described a young couple flush with happiness, who openly discussed their marriage set for June 14 and had invited him to be their best man. Everything was normal between his brother and Josephine when they left Edward and Maud's flat at 4:45 p.m. Herb was sober and Edward had never known him to touch alcoholic beverages.

In his cross-examination, Power sought to highlight for the court the lengthy engagement and the close relationship between the couple:

Q. … from sometime last fall you knew these two young people were engaged?

A. Yes, I knew.

Q. Did you know before the 17 of March that they had set the date of their marriage for June?

A. Yes, I heard them talk about it that they were going to get married in June, a couple of months before that.

Q. How did you observe your brother and Miss O'Brien behaving towards each other?

A. They seemed to be quite happy together as far as I could see.

Q. Would you say they were in love with each other?

A. Yes.

Q. Did you ever see them quarrel?

A. No.

Q. Did they appear to be happy?

A. Yes.

Q. Did you ever hear either one of them in the absence of the other make any complaint about the other's conduct or anything like that?

A. No.

Q. Josephine O'Brien was wearing an engagement ring?

A. Yes.

In emphasizing these points, Power hoped to establish in the jury's mind that the young couple had entered into a definite agreement to be married, a key element in his strategy to save Herb from the executioner.

The trial moved swiftly. On the first day, the crown called 16 witnesses, including the police officers who had been at the murder scene and those at the station who took the prisoner's statement in the early morning hours of March 18. Key to both the defence and the prosecution's case were the statements of those who had seen Spratt on the night of the murder.

In response to questioning from Emerson, Ray Spratt testified about the strange behaviour of his brother on the night in question: "He appeared to me to be a man under the influence of liquor—kind of staggering. His eyes seemed to be closed to me …" Theresa Spratt, along with Hubert and Terrence Murphy, also described similar encounters with Herb. Under cross-examination, all affirmed the bizarre behaviour of the accused.

Mr. and Mrs. Lynch and their five boarders, who occupied the upstairs flat on Plymouth Road, testified to hearing nothing from the flat downstairs on the night in question. In a written deposition to the court, Beatrice Tobin, a servant with Mrs. Lynch, stated that she was home upstairs all afternoon but had not gone downstairs after 5 p.m. She served the boarders tea at 6 p.m. and, though the radio was switched on then, it was not loud. Beatrice reported leaving the house at 8:30 p.m. and returning at 10:30 p.m. At no time had she heard or seen anything unusual from the floor below.

Day one of the trial had clearly established for the jury the sequence of events on that violent night. The testimony of family members confirmed that the defendant had confessed to killing Josephine. The challenge for the defence lay in establishing the groundwork for reducing a likely conviction of murder to one of manslaughter.

At the end of day one, Emerson indicated to the court that he would call only three more witnesses and would likely wind up the crown's case by noon the next day. In a gruesome twist on the old adage "saving the best for last," the prosecution would highlight the graphic details of the murder beginning at 10 a.m., April 28, with testimony from the chief coroner, the government pathologist, and the lead investigator.

The chief coroner, Dr. Thomas Anderson, was a respected and well-known physician in the city with a broad range of medical experience spanning 35 years. Anderson served as superintendent of the Hospital for Mental and Nervous Diseases in St. John's from 1930 to 1934. His considerable reputation as a skilled surgeon led to his later appointment as superintendent of the General Hospital. With the aid of large photographs of the body, taken at the morgue, he outlined in clinical terms the injuries to Josephine O'Brien that had resulted in her death:

> The external examination was taken first. She was lying (in the morgue) with her face covered with scaled or clotted blood. Her hair on the right side was especially matted together with blood. There was a bruise on her upper lip, and a bruise with a small cut on her lower lip, and an incisor tooth, i.e., one of her front teeth was broken off across. There were three decided incised wounds to the right of the ridge around her ear, extending down to the cheekbone. There were three distinct incisions there. Looking backwards towards the ear, the ear was sort of pulled downwards and forward, that is, the tissue to the skull was hauled away and there was a series of smashes in the bone behind the ear, that is a large open wound, in which bone fragments and bone tissue were coming out. Behind that towards the back of the skull there were three at least definite separate wounds, gaping open and the back one extending in where you could get fragments of bone and brain tissue coming out. There were bruises over her chest wall in front here and two or more bruises over her left shoulder area extending up to her neck. One of her fingernails had been torn off.

In response to cross-examination by Power, Anderson observed that the victim's fingernail would have been torn off by something with which she was struggling.

Dr. Joseph Edward Josephson took the stand next. He, too, was a respected member of the medical establishment in the city. Josephson, a graduate of Queen's University and the University of Toronto with a specialty in laboratory medicine, held certification from the Royal College of Physicians and Surgeons and was the Newfoundland government pathologist as well as being chief of clinical pathology at the General Hospital. Josephson estimated that death would have occurred six to eight hours prior to his arrival on the murder scene in the early hours of March 18, or likely between 4:30 and 6:30 p.m. on March 17. His examination of the victim's brain the next day in company with Anderson led him to conclude that the deep lacerations were caused by a heavy instrument, probably an iron. He reported that his examinations, both microscopic and otherwise, showed no evidence of pregnancy.

Carter also sought to clarify whether there was any evidence that Josephine had put up a prolonged struggle during the assault:

> Q. With reference to the blow to the mouth, what could cause that?
> A. Some dull instrument.
> Q. Could it be caused by a fist?
> A. Yes.
> Q. ... and assuming that the blow to the mouth was inflicted by a fist, and assuming that it was the first blow, would it be sufficient in your opinion to render a person unconscious?
> A. Yes, it could be, it must have been a fairly forcible blow to break off one of the teeth.

In addition to determining the cause of death, Josephson analyzed the bloodstains on clothing worn by Herb and by Josephine, evidence which he outlined in detail to the court. A blue suit jacket taken from Herb on the night of his arrest had no fewer than 50 bloodstains on the shoulder, around the lapels, and around the handkerchief pocket. Josephson's analysis showed that these stains were all human blood, identical to Josephine's blood type. The same was true of the bloodstains found on Herb's shirt, overshoes, hat, and necktie.

Cross-examined by Power as to how he had determined the time of death, Josephson indicated he had made an estimate based on the temperature in the room and the fact that post-mortem rigidity had just begun to set in. Power sought a more precise answer but other than a general agreement that the blows to Josephine's head were inflicted within a period of 60 seconds or so, Josephson shed no further light on the exact time of death.

Emerson called the final witness for the prosecution at 11:15 a.m. on April 28. Sergeant W.F. Case was no stranger to crime scenes and violence. After returning from World War I in 1919, he had joined the Newfoundland Constabulary and for the next 15 years served in various postings around Newfoundland. He received a promotion to sergeant with the force in 1935 along with a transfer to the CID in St. John's.

Case testified that he had arrived at 33 Plymouth Road shortly after midnight on March 18. He then proceeded to reconstruct the murder scene for the court.

Facing him as he entered the kitchen was the body of a young woman sprawled on a couch, her face completely covered in blood and with severe wounds on the side of her head. She was dead.

"Did you touch the body?" asked Emerson.

"I felt the right arm which was lying by the right side," said Case. "It was cold and stiff, indicating that the body was dead for some time. I noticed on touching the right arm that the hand was grasping a quantity of hair." Emerson appeared to ignore the statement.

The detective continued his testimony, indicating that the curtains on the window above the couch were drawn closed and pinned together. He noted that a lady's coat, hat, and a bloodstained white scarf crumpled in a ball lay on the kitchen table. Case told the court that he completed his investigation of the murder scene at 12:30 a.m. and issued a call for the arrest of Herbert Spratt.

Emerson then drew the court's attention to the statement made by Spratt after his arrest on the morning of March 18 at the CID office. He wanted to establish at the outset that police had not pressured Herb into making his statement:

Q. I want you to be very careful here, Sergeant. I don't

want any conversations between you and the accused that have no direct bearing on the subject.

A. He first spoke to me.

Q. We will leave it at that. What did you say to him in relation to the offence itself?

A. After a little conversation I spoke to him and told him about the body of Josephine O'Brien having been found at 33 Plymouth Road. I cautioned him, telling him he was suspected of having committed the murder of Josephine O'Brien, and that he was not bound to make any statement or say anything that would incriminate himself, but that if he desired to do so it would be taken down and used in evidence at his trial. He showed his intention of making a statement—said he wanted to make a statement …

Q. I would now ask to have that statement read.

A. (Witness reads statement): "Statement of Herbert Spratt after having been cautioned by Sergeant Case as follows":

… She, Josephine O'Brien, was off this evening. I was a Government Checker with the Canadian Government, and supposed to stay on the job. I always called her "Jo." She told me that she was having an evening off today so I went home today at twelve o'clock. I took the day off. We went for a little walk and then went back to my brother's, Edward Spratt, Plymouth Road. My brother Edward was home at the time. We remained five or ten minutes and then went for a little walk. We went down Water Street for a while and had a walk and then returned to my brother's house. There was no one home and the fire was out. There was no one in my brother's kitchen. We bought some ice cream before going in and sat down eating them. We intended going to a show at the Capitol but she was feeling kind of sick. We sat down there on the couch talking and kissed a bit like a fellow and girl are. We then lay down on the couch. We were talking about one thing and another, and she told me she was going to have a baby. She had my ring on her finger, my watch on her arm and my cross on her neck. I struck her with my fist and made a mark which is on my finger or I might have made it. I don't know if she fainted or if she went out but the little stove was right there. I filled up and I jumped, and the first thing I saw was an iron (electric) … I was a short distance away and she was on the couch. I am not sure if she was lying or sitting. She made a scream as I had the iron in my hand. I stopped for a second maybe I came to my senses and I struck her just once. I do not know if I struck her after that, all I know is she gave a groan, then I saw blood on the side and front of her face. I took my hat and my gloves. I think I took her scarf or mine. I left the scarf in some beer parlour. I went to different places. I don't know what happened after that. We were talking about getting married on June 14. That is when I was at the house first. I was at my brother's, 144 Water Street, when police found me. That is all. (Statement signed by the accused)

Emerson asked Case to show the jury each article of clothing taken from Spratt after his arrest. The blue suit coat worn by the accused on the night of the murder was placed in evidence as were the trousers, the vest, the tie, and the collar. Case described in detail the numerous bloodstains on each article.

It became obvious during Case's lengthy testimony that his investigative skills were beyond reproach. His precise observations of the crime scene created a vivid picture of the tragic events at 33 Plymouth Road on March 17. In one poignant exchange Emerson wanted to know what clothing Josephine was wearing:

A. On the body at the time was a blue sweater with buttons up the front where it was opened, a reddish or prune colored dress, silk stockings and black shoes.
Q. … the deceased was wearing a sweater which buttoned up the front. What kind of buttons were these?

A. They were blue buttons. I may state here that when making an examination of the premises on my arrival on that early morning, underneath the sideboard I picked up a blue button which is identical with the buttons on the sweater worn by the deceased. There was one button missing from that sweater.

Emerson did not want to leave any doubt in the jury's mind about the ferocious nature of the assault inflicted on Josephine O'Brien. In a dramatic climax he asked Case to describe other graphic details of the murder scene. Reading from his notes, Case highlighted what could only be seen as an act of horrific violence: "Blood marks on the wall extended five feet nine inches from the level of the couch. Blood spots extended across the dishes on the dresser to the electric washer eight feet distant. Other spots on the southeast corner of the room were ten feet from the head of the deceased. There was a streak of blood across the curtains showing they had been closed."

In a lengthy cross-examination of Case, Power established only that his client made no attempt to cover up his crime. The defence lawyer informed the court that for some six hours after the murder, during which Herb's whereabouts for the most part remained a mystery, he made no effort to change his bloodstained clothing nor had he made any effort to wash the victim's blood from his hands. When asked by police if he wished to make a statement, Herb had willingly co-operated and made a confession without any prompting from the officer.

In an unusual twist, before Case was excused, a juror requested the court's permission to seek clarification on one of the officer's earlier statements:

Q. My lord; Sergeant Case, you say on your visit to the home you found the body of the girl in that position with the right hand grasping a quantity of hair. Was that hair taken and examined to determine where it came from, if so, what was the result?
A. That hair was examined by Dr. Josephson, and as far as I can understand from Dr. Josephson, my lord, it was her own hair.

The exchange prompted Emerson to recall Josephson to the stand:

> Q. There was some hair found in the hand of the deceased?
> A. Yes.
> Q. Was that examined by you?
> A. Yes.
> Q. In comparison with her hair?
> A. Yes; I compared those hairs with the ones that I removed at the autopsy examination from her head. They compared favourably.
> Q. You were satisfied that the hair in her hand was her own hair?
> A. Yes.

With this final flourish, Emerson indicated to the court that the crown's case had concluded.

When court resumed at 2:30 p.m., Power opened his defence by calling his sole witness, Lieut. Kevin Maher, Records Officer with the Royal Canadian Navy in St. John's. In response to questioning, Maher confirmed Spratt's discharge from the Royal Navy and his repatriation on board HMS *Rodney*. He also confirmed the heavy engagement between the *Rodney* and the *Bismarck* during which the German battleship was sunk. There were no questions from the prosecution.

Maher had completed his testimony in 10 minutes and at 2:40 p.m. the counsel for the defence began his address to the jury without calling Spratt to the stand.

Power reviewed his client's actions on the evening of March 17 and asked the jury to consider the accused's mental state. He explained to them that Spratt had joined the Royal Navy believing himself to be in prime physical condition. After serving for only several months he was shocked by his diagnosis of pulmonary tuberculosis and the subsequent Admiralty ruling that he would be discharged from the Navy on medical grounds.

Power then advanced a defence of provocation, a defence that had been used in English courtrooms since the early 18th century when Chief

Justice Holt established instances where a charge of murder might be reduced to the lesser offence of manslaughter: angry words followed by an assault, seeing an Englishman being unlawfully deprived of his liberty, and seeing another man committing adultery with his wife. In the latter case, Holt had commented, "for jealousy is the rage of a man, and adultery is the highest invasion of property."

By the beginning of the early 1900s most countries within the British Empire recognized through their criminal codes that a wrongful act or insult could be powerful enough to deprive an ordinary person of the power of self-control. A murder thus committed in "the heat of passion," while not excusable, could be considered manslaughter.

Power's challenge was to convince the jury that his client had acted in the heat of passion. He begged the jury to understand that the girl to whom Spratt was engaged and with whom he was very much in love had that evening announced that she was pregnant. Knowing that he could not possibly be the father, Spratt had lost complete control of his senses. The girl's statement, he argued, had resulted in an explosion of blind rage from a man already suffering emotional upheaval from his war experiences. Counsel argued that the accused had provided a truthful statement to the police and there was no premeditation. In summation he stressed that he was not asking for an acquittal; he was asking that the charge of murder be reduced to one of manslaughter. Power completed his address to the jury at 3:25 p.m.

Emerson began his address to the jury immediately after, complimenting Power for his skilled defence, "as fine an effort as I have experienced in my thirty years at the bar." His patronizing words of praise for Power did not disguise his confidence in the outcome of the trial. He then launched into a vigorous assault on the weak defence, racking up the score against his opponent.

In summarizing the evidence, Emerson contended that the defence of provocation was based entirely on an unproven statement of the accused that the victim had told him she was pregnant. Even had there been solid evidence that the victim had made this statement, he argued, there was no basis for the reduction of the charge from murder to manslaughter. "English Law," he stated, "holds that a verdict of manslaughter may be brought in the case in which a man discovers his wife in the act of adultery." Emerson informed the jury that numerous precedents had established that this law does not apply in the case of an engaged couple.

Emerson next attacked the defence's argument that the accused was in a state of nervous abnormality when he viciously assaulted Josephine O'Brien with an iron, causing her death. It was not enough, he argued, to suggest that there was a mental disorder, but as in the case of a plea of insanity, it must be proven, and it was the responsibility of the defence to bring forward this proof. No solid evidence had been brought forward, he declared. It was therefore the crown's position that justice would only be served by a guilty verdict. Emerson thanked the jury, nodded to his lordship, and retired to his seat in the courtroom.

Emerson knew only too well where the eminent judge stood on the line of reasoning presented by the defence. In his charge to the jury, Horwood dealt at length with the issue of provocation. His words echoed those he had delivered in the same courtroom in November 1922, at the murder trial of Chinese immigrant Wo Fen Game. Ironically, Emerson had defended Wo Fen Game at the 1922 trial using the same provocation defence. Horwood's words at that trial indicated that he had little sympathy for the legal arguments used:

> There is no doubt as to the law on provocation. Provocation, sufficient to incite to kill must be gross, if it is to have the result of reducing the crime to manslaughter. Nothing short of a grave provocation is sufficient. Uncontrollable impulse is not a defence. Life would be very insecure if a slayer would say he killed his victim because of an uncontrollable impulse.
>
> To establish a defence on the grounds of insanity, it must be proved that at the time of the act the prisoner was labouring under a delusion so as not to know what he was doing or if he did wrong.

At the end of day two of Spratt's trial, the jury retired at 4:10 p.m. to consider the verdict. The deliberations were brief. After little more than 40 minutes, the 12 men returned to the courtroom. P.R. McCormac, foreman of the jury, stood and announced the verdict: "We find the prisoner guilty but in view of the prisoner's youth and indifferent health, as well as the fact that he served with a good record his King and country, we wish to couple with the verdict a serious and sincere recommendation of mercy at the hands of the law or the hands of the representative of His Majesty the King." The clerk of the court handed the chief justice the handwritten copy of the jury's recommendation for mercy.

Horwood only fleetingly glanced at the note before asking the prisoner to stand. "Herbert Augustus Spratt, you have been found guilty of the crime of murder. Do you have any reason why the sentence of this court should not be passed upon you?" Spratt stared blankly at the bench without responding. Horwood repeated the question. After an uneasy silence in the courtroom, he delivered the sentence:

> This court doth ordain you, Herbert Augustus Spratt, to be taken hence to the place from whence you came, and from thence to the place of execution, and that you be there hanged by the neck until you are dead: and that your body be afterwards buried within the precincts of the prison in which you shall have been confined after your conviction and may the Lord have mercy on your soul.

The prisoner staggered backwards, jolted by the impact of the judgment. A hushed silence filled the crowded courtroom as the High Sheriff handcuffed Spratt and led him away.

One trial had concluded at the Supreme Court but another was about to begin in the backrooms of Newfoundland's colonial government.

Four

Every prisoner condemned to death ... shall be
confined in a cell apart from all other prisoners,
and shall be placed by day and night under the
constant charge of a guard.

—Regulations for a Hanging,
Colony of Newfoundland, 1891

I n earlier and meaner times, when courts were held to be infallible,
executions followed closely on the heels of a conviction, often by no
more than a few days. In 1942, a three-week period of grace—including at least three Sundays—had become the norm within the British
justice system. Twenty-one days was still a short time between conviction
and execution.

The Commissioner of Justice scheduled an appointment with the
hangman for Friday at the stroke of 8 a.m., May 22, 1942. People in St.
John's would then be celebrating Empire Day weekend.

Power did not file an appeal on behalf of his client. After his lack-
lustre courtroom performance, the defence lawyer dropped out of sight,
and Herb Spratt was without representation. The convicted man's only
option was to await the outcome of the jury's recommendation of mercy—an appeal for clemency directly to the king's representative in Newfoundland, Governor Sir Humphrey Walwyn. In effect Walwyn would be
asked to invoke the Royal Prerogative, the ancient right of British mon-
archs to bestow mercy on convicted persons.

The authority to extend mercy in a case of capital punishment had
been passed to the governor by a set of royal instructions, known as
Letters Patent, issued by the British government in January 1934 after
Newfoundland suspended its constitution. Under the instructions to the
governor and commander-in-chief of the island of Newfoundland and

its dependencies, the Letters Patent authorized and empowered:

> Our said Governor as he shall see occasion, in Our name and Our behalf, to grant to any offender convicted of any crime in any court, or before any Judge, Justice or Magistrate within our said Island, a pardon, either free or subject to lawful conditions; Now We do hereby direct and enjoin our said Governor to call upon the judge who presided at the trial of any offender who shall have been condemned to suffer death by the sentence of any Court ... to make to our said Governor a written report of the case of such offender, and such report of the said judge shall ... be taken in consideration ...

To fully comply with the royal instructions, the governor was required to consult with the Commission of Government, the six men appointed by the British Dominions Office to govern Newfoundland. Clearly, however, the governor was to merely seek advice and make his own decision, whether the six men agreed or not.

Humphrey Thomas Walwyn was born into an upper-class English military family in 1879. At the age of 14 he entered the prestigious Britannia Royal Military College in Devon and, for the next 40 years as a Royal Navy officer, he knew only a life of command, control, and stiff-upper-lip British discipline. In February 1936, having recently retired from his naval career, he accepted an appointment as governor and commander-in-chief over the island of Newfoundland and its dependencies. He brought with him to "grimy" St. John's the imperial upper-class attitudes of the time, coupled with a mindset that he was captain of the ship in this reminted British colony.

The Commissioner of Natural Resources in the colony, Sir John Hope Simpson, described Walwyn as "an admiral with a fine quarterdeck manner and an astonishingly free use of the broadside." In comparing him to the previous governor, Hope Simpson somewhat uncharitably portrayed the new representative of the king as "much more unpleasant and extraordinarily vigorous and impetuous—and stupid." Walwyn was spit and polish and never missed an opportunity to don the uniform that displayed his rank as an admiral in the Royal Navy.

Attorney General Emerson, in his role as Commissioner of Justice, notified Walwyn by letter on April 29 that the trial had concluded and a death sentence from Chief Justice Horwood, along with a strong recommendation for mercy from the jury, had been the outcome. In response, the governor suggested a short meeting to review the case and outlined a series of questions he needed answered before he made a decision:

1. What was Herbert Spratt's naval record?
2. What is his medical record now?
3. Is he the same lad who held up a shopkeeper with a toy pistol before the war?
4. Is there any insanity in his family?
5. What sort of upbringing did he have?
6. What are his parents like?
7. Where was he brought up?
8. Did he go to school?

On the morning of Monday, May 4, Emerson arrived at the Colonial Building on Military Road in St. John's to brief Walwyn prior to a full session of the Commission of Government. In a long and detailed report, he schooled the governor on the reasoning behind the jury's verdict and the court's sentence.

Emerson opened his presentation by questioning the strategies used by Power in the defence of Herbert Spratt, maintaining that, through his considerable connections in the city, he learned prior to the trial that Power had intended to prove that the accused was insane in law. Emerson explained that under the M'Naghten Rules established by the House of Lords in the United Kingdom in 1843 Power would have to prove that his client suffered from a disease of the mind at the time of the alleged murder and therefore he did not know what he was doing and that it was wrong. A successful defence under these rules meant that his client would likely spend the rest of his life in an insane asylum as had happened in the case of Francis Oxford when he was declared not guilty by reason of insanity in the killing of his girlfriend at King's Point, Newfoundland, in 1931.

According to Emerson, Power abandoned the insanity defence before the trial under pressure from the elder Spratt, who under no circumstances wanted the stigma of mental illness attached to the family name. As an alternative, Power decided to plead for a reduced sentence of manslaughter based on provocation. Emerson stressed that his "considerable connections" also informed him that the defence lawyer intended to boost his case by showing that Herb Spratt's actions were aggravated by a condition of nervous abnormality brought on by his war experiences. "If a person was suffering from such a mental condition, this alone would justify a reduction of the sentence," Emerson asserted, "but none of this was proven by any form of evidence presented at the trial."

In fact, argued Emerson, the opposite was the case. There was nothing to suggest that Spratt suffered from such a mental condition. He was calm and collected from the beginning. During the preliminary inquiry conducted by Magistrate O'Neill at the end of March, Spratt had displayed emotion only when he was shown photographs of the deceased. Emerson stated, "During the trial itself on the 27 and 28, it was impossible for me to note the demeanor of the accused as he sat at the back of the court. I am informed, however, that he was calm and collected throughout." The governor was left with the clear impression that the justice system was dealing with a cold-blooded killer who felt no remorse for his crime.

Emerson then outlined that the defence plea of provocation—Josephine's statement that she was pregnant—was bound to fail: "Some judges have held that a sudden confession to an unsuspecting husband of adulterous intercourse by his wife is equivalent to a discovery of 'in flagrante delicto.'" It was the same as the husband's catching his wife in the act. Emerson outlined a number of legal cases where courts had made a ruling of manslaughter in situations where the husband had lost total control and killed his wife after she had confessed to adultery. All courts, he stressed, have ruled that these precedents did not apply in cases of engaged couples and therefore could not be used to grant a pardon.

Referring to the request for mercy, Emerson cautioned the governor that "[t]he jury's mind is not necessarily logical" and, while he admitted the youth of the accused could be taken into consideration, he stressed that factors such as poor health and a good military record were no grounds for granting a pardon. He asked the governor to note, as well, that the jury made no reference to mental instability in their plea for mercy.

In response to the governor's questions on the Spratt family, Emerson held nothing back in detouring around the facts of the case into the realm of hearsay and innuendo. "I have certain information," he informed the governor, "which satisfies me that in considering their verdict (a) certain jurors expressed opinions against the imposition of the death penalty and it may be that they would not have voted for a verdict of murder unless it was coupled with a strong recommendation for mercy and (b) Some jurors, knowing the accused's father (as everybody does) and considering the ferocity of the attack, were of the opinion that he is a boy of mental instability."

Emerson acknowledged that the accused had been brought up in a respectable household within a family of moderate means. Then, in a gossipy tone, he continued: "The father is Councillor Spratt, who suffers from egocentricity in a marked degree. It is probable the accused has inherited this mental instability. He does not however appear to be vicious." Emerson's deliberate smears against Councillor Spratt's character revealed his attitudes toward a person he viewed as a working-class hero in the city, one with whom he had crossed swords on several occasions.

In considering the weight of the jury's recommendation for mercy, Emerson asked the governor to consider the attitude on the street: "What has been picked up by legal members of my department is a general view that Spratt should be hanged. I do not forget the limits of the circles in which I and my informants move nor do I forget that public opinion is very fickle."

In an ironic forewarning of what was to happen in the case of Alfred Beaton only a few years later, Emerson cautioned that negative public reaction and criticism would be levelled at the governor if the execution was carried out. Emerson reminded Walwyn that Councillor Spratt was a popular figure among the working class of the city: "We might even find His Excellency will be presented with a petition signed by vast numbers seeking remission of the extreme penalty. I hear that the GWVA [Great War Veterans Association] recently considered the case and decided to postpone their decision for the present."

As a final point, Emerson offered Walwyn a scrap of wiggle room. The governor might want to consider, he suggested, whether this was a crime of passion as opposed to a violent offence committed with pre-meditation. In such case, Walwyn could think about the possibility of exercising the Royal Prerogative.

Emerson concluded his presentation with a footnote on the recent history of capital punishment in Newfoundland, noting that "this was the only white man to be convicted of murder in Newfoundland since 1899 and only one other case occurred, that of a Chinaman who became berserk in 1925 and after purchasing a revolver shot dead three of his compatriots and then turned the revolver on himself, without success." He highlighted his own role as defence counsel in the Wo Fen Game case, but in an uncharacteristic lapse of memory he provided the wrong dates for the trial and execution which had occurred just before Christmas in 1922.

Walwyn thanked Emerson for his comprehensive report and guidance but did not indicate his likely course of action. As follow-up he requested medical reports from experts on mental illness as well as a report from the prison superintendent.

In line with Walwyn's wishes, Emerson asked for a medical report on the prisoner from Dr. Thomas Anderson, superintendent of the General Hospital. The report, submitted jointly by Dr. Anderson and Dr. E. Leo Sharpe, prison physician, arrived in Emerson's office in the late afternoon of May 4, 1942. The two respected doctors had examined Spratt the previous day and recorded serious doubts about his mental stability and sanity. Physically they found the prisoner "frail, excitable, and ill-disciplined." He appeared abnormally listless and resigned to his execution.

In a discussion about the prisoner's previous mental history, the doctors revealed that when Spratt was being treated for tuberculosis in a sanitorium in England from December 16, 1940, to May 17, 1941, he experienced visions of being part of a brotherhood. The hallucinations bothered him so much that he sought the advice of a spiritual advisor.

The report disclosed another disturbing incident which became a prelude to the tragedy. One night, about a month before the murder, Spratt had picked up an iron after Josephine had refused intimacy. She was lying on the couch with her eyes closed. He had stood over her with the iron in his hand, but this time controlled the impulse. She had opened her eyes and asked him if he had been going to strike her. He could not recall his response.

On the night of the murder the prisoner remembered hitting Josephine in the mouth and chin. He could not recall inflicting any wounds, but remembered blood on his cheek.

The doctors expressed their professional conclusions: "this fact (failed memory) is indicative of a 'brain storm' or uncontrollable violent impulse. The possibility and probability of mental disease called Schizo-phrenia or 'divided personality' must be considered."

On the same day a memo from the superintendent of His Majesty's Penitentiary supported the concerns expressed in the medical report of Anderson and Sharpe. Superintendent Byrne reported that prior to trial the prisoner had repeatedly tried to injure himself by banging his head violently against the stone wall of his cell. He was also subject to intense headaches, fits of hysteria, and violent trembling. Sometimes these attacks were so severe that guards had to strap him to a bed. After his sentencing, Spratt "was extraordinarily calm and somewhat dazed." Otherwise, Byrne said, the prisoner had given no trouble and spent his days reading, sleeping, and quietly pacing his cell.

Byrne's memo along with the Anderson/Sharpe medical report was sharply at odds with the line of thinking promulgated by Emerson that the prisoner was a calm, remorseless killer who had shown no emotion at his trial. Emerson had already made up his mind that Spratt must hang. He rejected the diagnosis offered by the doctors and dismissed their expert opinions out of hand. "The value of this report did not appeal to me," he informed the governor, "so I requested Dr. Grieve to visit and examine the prisoner."

The meeting between Dr. Grieve, the current superintendent of the Hospital for Mental and Nervous Diseases, and the condemned man took place in Byrne's office on May 6. According to Grieve, the behaviour of the prisoner brought to the office was a far cry from what had been described in the earlier report. According to the Grieve, Spratt's behaviour remained normal throughout the meeting.

On May 7, Grieve delivered the opinion that Emerson wanted, stating that Spratt was "even tempered, pleasant and cooperative, had a friendly manner, was coherent, and displayed no delusions or hallucinations ..." When asked about the murder, Spratt was "unable to explain the emotional outburst that ended in the death of Miss O'Brien." Grieve saw no sign of mental deficiency or illness.

As additional evidence of the convicted man's callous attitude, Emerson attached a copy of a letter written by Spratt the day before the trial to an ex-girlfriend, Mary Burke:

Dear Mary,

You will no doubt be surprised to receive a letter from me, but you are the only one I can really call a friend. I didn't put my address in the top of this letter, as you know where I am (right opposite the hospital). There is no reason why you should worry your pretty head over me, but if I could only see you for a few minutes there is something I want to ask you. If you can't get down in the day, you may be able to in the night, come about seven o'clock or 7:30 and ask for Mr. Mullett or Mr. Morris. I'm sure they will let me see you for a few minutes. Better still ask for Mr. Divine, he's the head man and he's very good to me. I don't want to tell you on paper Mary, but if you don't want to come, please write me. It is going to mean my future Mary, so don't let me down. Remember no matter what happened between us, we always came back to each other, or is that all over now? We were both engaged you know. And Mary there is a reason for doing "Everything." Visiting days are on Monday between two and four.

But if you can't make it then try some night or other day that you are off. You don't have to bring a thing Mary just yourself. I got some nerve I know (if you could see me now, you wouldn't say that) writing to you like this but I'm hoping for the best. I'm not forgetting what Vic told me, that's why I sent you a birthday card.

I'm keeping my fingers crossed.
Herb (Spratt)

P.S. Is it too-o-o-o late now Mary?

"I do not know," said Emerson, "whether anything can be inferred as to the mentality of a man who under the circumstances such as existed then, could write such a letter."

After his meeting with Emerson on the morning of May 4, Walwyn anxiously awaited a report from the chief justice. On May 5 Horwood's legal opinion arrived and it was obvious immediately that he was in no mood for mercy. "I have to report that there cannot be any question as to the correctness of the verdict of guilty," he stated. "I told the jury when they returned that it was the only verdict they could have found upon the evidence."

Horwood believed the crown's case had been proven beyond any doubt. The prisoner had admitted to the murder and the only conflict in Spratt's statement revolved around the alleged pregnancy of Miss O'Brien, which had been refuted by expert testimony at trial. Horwood believed that Spratt was lying and found it "highly improbable that for no apparent reason she was falsely accusing herself of immorality ... this [he] consider[ed] to be so absurd as to be unbelievable."

Horwood questioned why the prisoner had not taken the stand and given his testimony under oath. He also noted that, from the time the murder was committed to the time that Spratt had showed up at his brother's home on Water Street, five hours had elapsed, certainly plenty of time for the accused to consult with others and decide what he could say in a confession he might give to police. Since no such evidence of conspiracy came out of the police investigation or emerged at the trial, Horwood was engaging in speculation. Even so, the piling on of doubt further damaged the chances of clemency for Spratt.

Horwood was unflinching in his recommendation to Walwyn: "There is nothing that I have to suggest that might be considered by Your Excellency as grounds for the exercise of The Royal Prerogative."

On Friday, May 8, zero hour for Herb Spratt was just two weeks away. The final countdown began at 10 a.m. when Walwyn convened a meeting of the Commission of Government at the Colonial Building to discuss the question of clemency. The most powerful people in the land were in attendance: Lewis Edward Emerson, Commissioner of Justice and Defence and chief prosecutor at the trial; Peter Douglas Dunn, Commissioner of

Natural Resources; Ira Wild, Commissioner of Finance; Harry A. Winter, Commissioner of Home Affairs and Education; Sir Wilfred Woods, Commissioner of Public Utilities; and John C. Puddester, Commissioner of Health and Welfare. No one represented the convicted man.

Emerson presented the case against Spratt and, after a short discussion, the Commission unanimously agreed that the execution should proceed. In a recorded motion the commissioners advised the governor "that he should not grant a pardon or reprieve or interfere with the sentence imposed on the accused by the Supreme Court."

Walwyn accepted the advice. As he was a military man, it would have been out of character for him to overturn a decision of those around him whom he considered his staff officers. The commissioners turned their attention to the next item on the agenda; even the building of the scaffold was government business and the Commission approved the expenditure of $18.50 in overtime for the carpenter hired by the police.

At Emerson's request, Walwyn convened a second meeting at the Colonial Building on Saturday, May 9, at 12:30 p.m. to deal with routine items related to the execution. Emerson chose his words carefully during the discussion and advised the commissioners that he had considered two options in the search for an executioner. One was to recruit a person from the local population, and the other was to engage the services of a prisoner at the penitentiary. He informed his colleagues that he had discarded both options. "For certain reasons I considered it inadvisable," said Emerson, "and accordingly I have asked Canadian authorities if they could make the services of an appropriate official available for the purpose."

The commissioners indicated their agreement and Emerson outlined the remaining steps before the hanging, set for Friday, May 22. He would inform the superintendent of His Majesty's Penitentiary, the High Sheriff of Newfoundland, the prisoner, and the prisoner's counsel of the governor's decision. A press release would then be prepared for the governor's office. The meeting adjourned at 1:30 p.m.

Walwyn and Emerson still suspected that a controversy would erupt out of the great silence that had settled over the affair in St. John's. The two men fully expected that someone would launch a public appeal for mercy—possibly Councillor James Spratt and his many supporters, or the Great War Veterans Association. Perhaps they would launch an appeal directly to the British government and the king. To block any potential backdoor petition, Walwyn sent a telegram to the Secretary of State for Dominion Affairs in London to express the finality of his ruling:

> Herbert A. Spratt was on April 28 sentenced to death by Supreme Court for brutal murder of a girl aged about twenty. Jury coupled with verdict a serious and sincere recommendation for mercy. Commission unanimous that recommendation not be acceded to. Chief Justice who tried case is strongly of same opinion. Independently of these opinions I have decided not to interfere with carrying out of sentence. Foregoing is for your information in case you are approached for a reprieve.

The stage was set for the second execution of the 20th century in Newfoundland.

With Sir Humphrey Walwyn's decision not to interfere, the Newfoundland government had almost washed its hands of the affair. But another thorny issue surfaced on May 18 when the governor's office received a request that Spratt's body be turned over to his parents for burial in consecrated ground.

Walwyn convened another session of the Commission on May 19 at 10 a.m. to consider the request. The meeting was a stormy affair with Emerson arguing that the letter of the law must be observed and the body—being the property of the state—must be buried within the penitentiary walls. The others around the table supported a more compassionate response and maintained that allowing family members or representatives of the church to take possession of the body was now common practice in the Dominion of Canada and elsewhere. In the end, over Emerson's strong objections, the commissioners agreed "to advise His Excellency the Governor that he should be pleased to modify the sentence passed upon Herbert Spratt by the Supreme Court to permit of the body, after execution of the sentence, being passed over to the parents for burial."

The action now shifted to His Majesty's Penitentiary on Forest Road. Several days earlier the carpenter's pounding hammer and his raspy handsaw broke the morning quiet at the prison. The scaffold began to rise from the dusty ground at the northeast end of the prison yard.

An observer at the 1922 execution of Wo Fen Game in St. John's provided a vivid picture of the execution platform, built to government standard: "an ordinary platform, twelve feet by twelve feet built of matched board. It was raised about four feet from the ground, with the sides boarded up, except for a doorway in one side. The door to the side was for the purpose of removing the body from the pit." Directly underneath the trap door of the platform, prison staff excavated a trench, 8 feet deep to ensure that the hanged man's feet did not touch ground. The platform was a practical, sturdy affair, "surrounded by a guardrail of two by four scantling. At two sides rose two pieces of four by four studding, on top of which was nailed a stout crossbar somewhat after the style of an ordinary swing."

Herb Spratt's execution was firmly set for Friday, May 22, at 8 a.m. The prisoner had a little over 48 hours to live.

Only scanty records document Spratt's behaviour as he endured the final hours before his hanging. Officials at the penitentiary fed a general statement to one reporter that "during his time there, his conduct was exemplary." Another paper, quoting "sources," stated, "during this time, he frequently expressed sorrow for his crime and his willingness to pay the death penalty." These standard official statements were designed to soothe the public mind and to indicate that the prisoner was a willing participant in his own execution.

Byrne, who spent many hours with the condemned man in his cell, reported to the Commissioner of Justice that the prisoner, calm and resigned to his fate, "now spends his time sleeping, reading and quietly pacing."

On May 21 a public notice was posted on the gate of His Majesty's Penitentiary:

> Whereas on the twenty-eighth day of April A.D. 1942, Herbert Augustus Spratt, upon conviction for murder, was sentenced to death by the Supreme Court of Newfoundland now we do hereby give public notice that the hour of eight o'clock of the morning of the twenty-second of May 1942 has been appointed for the execution of the said Herbert Augustus Spratt.

It was signed by John Cahill, High Sheriff of Newfoundland, and by G.G. Byrne, superintendent of the Penitentiary.

At 6 a.m. on May 22, Rev. Father Power of St. Joseph's Parish entered Spratt's cell and administered the last rites. The young man was outwardly calm and accompanied the two wardens of the death watch and the priest to Byrne's office. He was given time to write letters to his parents and to the O'Brien family in which he expressed sorrow for his crime. He had final words with his wardens and thanked the staff of the penitentiary for their kindnesses. The wardens then escorted the prisoner back to his cell.

At precisely 7:57 a.m., the executioner, a professional hangman from Canada, entered the cell, shook hands with the prisoner, and efficiently fastened a broad leather body belt around his waist and chest. His arms were then pinioned behind his back with two attached leather straps just above the elbows. His wrists were strapped with another attached belt. The ceremony of execution had begun.

The procession formed up for the short walk to the scaffold: Byrne in the lead; then Father Power, reciting the service for the burial of the dead; Herbert Spratt, the prisoner, calm and resigned to his fate; followed by the hangman, Sheriff Cahill, and Dr. Sharpe. Two wardens, Lush and Morris, flanked the prisoner.

After mounting the 10 steps leading to the scaffold, the hangman positioned Spratt over a line chalked on the trap door directly underneath the coiled noose.

The science of hanging—executioners preferred to call it an art—had long since been perfected, especially so in the United Kingdom, where that country's most famous hangman, James Berry, had carefully worked out a formula to calculate the length of drop required in feet and inches for a person of a specific body weight minus the estimated weight of the victim's head. "Length of drop, in feet, is found by dividing the number 539 by the square of the number of stones in weight [one stone equals 14 lbs.] of the convict's body, exclusive of the weight of his head." For example, a person of 168 pounds (minus the head) would need to drop 3 feet 9 inches.

Berry's modus operandi, largely copied throughout the British Empire, included "the most suitable class of rope … made of the finest Italian hemp, three quarters of an inch in thickness … Before using a rope for an execution, [he] thoroughly test[ed] it with bags of cement of about the weight of the condemned person, and this preliminary testing stretches the cord and at the same time reduces its diameter to five eighths of an inch."

In theory, the execution became a fail-safe procedure for severing the spinal column between the first and second vertebrae, pinching off the jugular vein, and causing strangulation. When the hangman bound the prisoner's arms and legs, when the noose was properly adjusted around the neck, and when the trap was sprung, the victim was launched into eternity within a matter of seconds. In the 20th century, with minor adjustments from time to time, the method became government standard.

But this scientific method was subject to human foibles. Even the most sober of hangmen, of which Berry was one, made mistakes in their calculations. In one of Berry's "terrible experiences," that of Robert Goodale on November 30, 1885, he miscalculated the length of the drop required to kill the overweight prisoner. "I pulled the lever … and the culprit dropped out of sight," said Berry. But then the empty (and very bloody) noose snapped back through the hole nearly hitting the witnesses on the scaffold.

"I thought that the noose had slipped from the culprit's head," said Berry, "but it was worse than that, for the jerk had severed the head entirely from the body, and both had fallen together to the bottom of the pit. We were all unnerved and shocked … the Governor (of the prison) … broke down and wept." It became known in hangman's lore as "the Goodale mess."

Botched hangings became a regular occurrence in the Dominion of Canada. When a severely disturbed Benny Swim murdered his ex-girlfriend and her new husband near Woodstock, New Brunswick, in 1922, he was duly convicted and sentenced to hang. Unfortunately, the sheriff of Woodstock encountered great difficulty in locating a competent executioner but finally settled on Mr. Doyle, a resident of Montreal, with a checkered past and a love for strong drink. Just in case anything went wrong, the sheriff insisted that Doyle bring a backup.

On execution day everything seemed to be going according to plan. The sheriff noticed that, although Doyle fumbled a bit, he managed to spring the trap just as Benny was in the middle of the Lord's Prayer. The prisoner dropped out of sight and witnesses heard a loud thump as the body hit the side of the gallows. After five minutes, the witnesses on the scaffold along with the hangman went below to check. "He's dead as a doornail," slurred Doyle. After the sheriff cut the body down, the three attending doctors discovered that the neck had merely been dislocated, and to everyone's horror, Benny began making gasping sounds. His pulse grew stronger by the minute and his chest began to heave. Two of the doctors panicked and hurriedly left the scene. Hangman Doyle was ordered from the prison.

After an hour the sheriff instructed the backup executioner, Mr. Gill, to hang Benny again. Supported by two men of the cloth, Benny was dragged back to the scaffold and hanged a second time.

Doyle's career ended after the double hanging of Benny Swim; however, bungled executions continued to happen regularly. Even the skills of Arthur Ellis, the most prominent member of Canada's corps of hangmen, began to erode around 1920, and his competence continued a downhill slide over the next 15 years. Among his most spectacular failures were the decapitations of Dan Prociev at Headingley Gaol in Manitoba in 1926 and of Tommasina Teolis at the Bordeaux Gaol in Montreal in 1935. The latter incident ended his career.

On the scaffold at His Majesty's Penitentiary in St. John's, the hangman turned to face Sheriff Cahill, who handed him a folded document bearing Cahill's signature officially authorizing the execution. The unmasked hangman then proceeded efficiently with his grim task. He pulled a white hood over the prisoner's head, fastened a leather strap around his legs just below the knees, and adjusted the noose so that the metal ring was just behind the left ear. A leather washer was pulled in behind the ring to prevent slippage. The prison bell began to toll.

A few seconds before 8 a.m. Father Power recited the last lines of his prayer, "Our Father, who art in heaven, hallowed be thy Name.... Amen and may the Lord Jesus protect you and lead you to eternal life." The hangman pulled the lever and the trap door fell away with a heavy crump which echoed through the spring morning. The chief warden hoisted the black flag over the penitentiary gate, indicating to the few people waiting outside that the execution had been carried out.

Sharpe conducted his medical examination of the body one hour later and issued a death certificate. The body of Herbert Augustus Spratt, in a simple wooden coffin, was handed over to his family outside the prison gate on Forest Road at 10 a.m.

Next day, the overcrowded Trouter's Special left the railway station in downtown St. John's and chugged along the overland route as far as Nine Mile Pond, dropping anglers off at their favourite fishing holes along the way. The Red Triangle Club on Water Street welcomed a record 3,160 servicemen and local citizens to enjoy the entertainment and good food throughout the weekend. At St. Patrick's Parish Hall, a local band played to a capacity crowd for the Empire Day dance.

The *Evening Telegram* devoted a short column on page 3 to the drama which had played out in the early morning hours of May 22 at the penitentiary. Much more space in an adjoining column was devoted to the conviction under the Highway Traffic Act of a Canadian soldier, Major Thomas Creighton, for killing a farmer's dog. The banner headline of the *Daily News*, the city's second-largest newspaper, indicated that the Russians were progressing on the Kharkov Front. A letter to the editor warned of the danger of sending matches through the mail.

Herb and Josephine during a visit to her parents in Cape Broyle in the fall of 1941. *Courtesy of Beverly O'Brien*

Josephine with her favourite pet, Topsy. *Courtesy of Beverly O'Brien*

St. John's in the early 1940s. Empire Avenue cuts diagonally across the lower half of the photo. *Photograph No. HD-28, reprinted by permission of the Government of Newfoundland and Labrador*

Gunner manning the Hill O'Chips/Water Street gun during World War II. Devon Row is in the background. *City of St. John's Archives, 01-45-008*

Front view of corvettes berthed abreast on the south side of St. John's Harbour during World War II. *City of St. John's Archives, 01-45-004*

Sir Lewis Edward Emerson (1890–1949). Under the Commission of Government, Emerson was Commissioner of Justice and Defence from 1940 to 1944. He became Chief Justice of the Newfoundland Supreme Court in 1944. *The Rooms Provincial Archives Division, E 32-26*

Sir William H. Horwood, chief justice of the Newfoundland Supreme Court, 1902–44. *The Rooms Provincial Archives Division, VA 33-6*

The Colonial Building, St. John's, 1940s, the seat of power for the Commission of Government. *The Rooms Provincial Archives Division, VA 3-8*

An early photo of Captain Gerald Guy Byrne in his Royal Newfoundland Regiment uniform. In 1942 he was superintendent of His Majesty's Penitentiary.
The Rooms Provincial Archives Division, 0-31.3

Sir Humphrey Thomas Walwyn, governor of Newfoundland, 1936–46, on the steps of the Colonial Building. *The Rooms Provincial Archives Division, A 2-100*

Sir Humphrey and Lady Walwyn bid goodbye to well-wishers at the railway station in St. John's on January 17, 1946. He retired to Dorset, England. *The Rooms Provincial Archives Division, A 8-33*

St. John's City Council 1945–49. Left to right: City Engineer Grant Jack, Oliver Vardy, Deputy Mayor James Spratt, John Kelly (standing), Mayor Andrew Carnell, Secretary Miss M. Ruby, Harry Mews, City Clerk John Mahoney (standing), William Ryan, and Eric Jerrett. *City of St. John's Archives, 06-02-026*

Inspector W.F. Case of the Newfoundland Constabulary and superintendent of His Majesty's Penitentiary 1944–65. *Courtesy of Capt. D. Harvey, HMP*

Five

All the world's a stage,
And all the men and women merely players:
They have their exits and their entrances;
—William Shakespeare

T he execution of Herbert Spratt did not register in the public mind and the event was quickly forgotten in the colony. The timing, on a holiday weekend, without press coverage, ensured that Emerson's fears of a public outcry did not materialize. The official notice of the hanging nailed to the prison gates drew only a few curious reporters.

But the event would claim another victim. Capt. Gerald Byrne had been superintendent of His Majesty's Penitentiary for 10 years when Spratt came to the prison in March 1942. Byrne developed a close relationship with the convicted man in the three weeks before the hanging. Each day he visited Spratt in his cell, observing his failing health as a result of a relapse of tuberculosis and the mental torture of sitting on death row. Under these circumstances, Byrne provided care and counselling beyond what was expected.

Byrne was an exceptional individual. When war came in August 1914, he volunteered immediately for the First Newfoundland Regiment. He was one of the famous First 500 soldiers who shipped out on the *Florizel* for the battlefields of Europe in October of that year.

British officers at the training base in Edinburgh recognized Byrne's leadership skills and initiative immediately and within a year he was promoted through the ranks to sergeant. Within another year he would be attending officer training in Camp Aldershot near London.

Between August and December 1915, Byrne fought with his regiment during the bitter campaign to seize the Gallipoli Peninsula from Turkey. Wounded and desperately ill with dysentery, he was evacuated to a hospital in Malta before the ill-fated campaign ended in early January 1916.

Byrne recovered and rejoined the 1st Newfoundland Regiment in time for the "Great July Drive" scheduled for July 1, 1916. On that tragic day in the fields of northern France near the village of Beaumont Hamel, most of his regiment was annihilated. Byrne was again wounded while leading his squadron into the storm of enemy fire.

On March 3, 1917, the regiment occupied trenches at Sailly-Saillisel, near the town of Albert and a stone's throw from the German trenches. A determined enemy launched an offensive which threatened to overwhelm the Newfoundland sector. With a small band of soldiers, Lieut. Byrne led a countercharge that drove the enemy back and prevented a breakthrough which would have endangered the whole Allied line. For his conspicuous gallantry, he received the Military Cross.

Byrne's distinguished war record paved the way for various jobs in the Dominion of Newfoundland public service after the war. In 1933 Prime Minister Alderdice approved his appointment as superintendent of His Majesty's Penitentiary in St. John's. The hanging of Herb Spratt would be his first experience with the execution of a prisoner.

By May 20, two days before the execution, construction of the scaffold had been completed at His Majesty's Penitentiary. An oppressive silence replaced the scraping of shovels in rocky ground as workers finished excavation of the pit. The carpenter laid down his hammer and saw, reminding inmates and wardens alike that the hanging was imminent. Tensions held the captive audience in an ever-tightening vice. The psychological impact on everyone at the prison, not well understood at the time, was to be felt far into the future.

In the early morning of May 22, 1942, Byrne shook the hand of Herb Spratt and said goodbye. He then led the procession to the scaffold, watched as the hangman performed his grisly task, and witnessed the strangulation of the young man at the end of a rope.

By early 1943, Byrne's health had deteriorated and his doctor diagnosed bleeding ulcers. There was little doubt that he was suffering from severe stress. Understandably, his performance as superintendent of the penitentiary suffered as a result. No such understanding would come from the Commissioner of Justice.

Emerson reported to Governor Walwyn that, up to 1942, Byrne had given excellent service and discharged his duties "with energy, ability and satisfaction." Since then, according to Emerson, conditions had worsened at the prison. Inmates were fighting. There were staff conflicts, lax discipline, and low morale.

Emerson charged that Byrne was often absent without permission and rumours of alcohol abuse persisted. Byrne defended himself as best he could and laid the blame for problems at His Majesty's Penitentiary squarely at the door of a penny-pinching Commission of Government which refused to allocate funding to address issues of decaying infrastructure and staff morale.

By the spring of 1944 communication between the two men had broken down completely and Emerson convinced his colleagues and Walwyn that a new head was needed at the prison. Byrne was suspended for neglect of duty and in August was forced into compulsory retirement on a pension of just over $1,100 per year. He was 54 years old, in poor health, and without the strength to continue the battle.

District Inspector Case (formerly Sergeant Case) of the Newfoundland Constabulary was appointed on an acting basis to replace Byrne. Within a few months he asked to be transferred back to the Constabulary unless money was allocated to correct the appalling conditions at the prison.

In the meantime Emerson cast about for a "suitable" prison superintendent. He had little confidence that anyone in Newfoundland could handle the job and asked Lord Cranborne at the Dominions Office in London to find suitable candidates with British colonial experience in the prisons of Africa or India. When no such candidates came forward, Case was confirmed in the position on September 1, 1945.

While the conflict played out at the penitentiary, other major changes occurred on the legal and political scene. In late September 1944, Chief Justice Horwood, declining in health at the age of 82, indicated to Walwyn that he wished to resign his post. He had presided over the Supreme Court for over 42 years and had been a commanding presence in the legal and political community in Newfoundland since 1885.

In the governor's eyes the logical successor to Horwood was the recently knighted Sir Lewis Edward Emerson, the Commissioner of Justice and Defence since 1937. On October 3, 1944, at 11 a.m., the fall session of the Supreme Court convened with Emerson in the chair. A large gathering of the city's elite watched as Horwood administered the oaths of allegiance and office, then turned and left the courtroom forever.

Six months later Horwood died at the General Hospital after a short illness. His funeral on April 9, 1945, at the Anglican Cathedral in St. John's drew the cream of the city's legal and business community. He was laid to rest at the Anglican Cemetery on Forest Road.

By September 1944, the first faint breezes of dramatic change began to ripple across Newfoundland. The war which had dominated life across the island for six years would soon grind to an end as German forces collapsed in Europe. Residents of the city began to breathe easier and turn to more pleasant thoughts.

On September 1, 1944, the *Evening Telegram* reported on the gala opening of the new Paramount Theatre on Harvey Road. Hundreds of city residents lined up outside to watch as Mayor Carnell cut the ceremonial ribbon. Walwyn, in his finest naval uniform, addressed the huge gathering of military and civilian dignitaries inside the 1,300-seat building. He praised the spacious air-conditioned theatre as "a showplace of Newfoundland" and "as good or better than any in Canada." The speeches gave way to the first movie at the Paramount, *Broadway Rhythm*, a Technicolor feature starring George Murphy and Ginny Simms.

With a formal end to the war in September 1945, Newfoundlanders showed the first indications of awakening from their political hibernation. The long sleep which began at the end of 1933 had now lasted for 12 years. Letters to the editor in major papers across the island began a debate over confederation with Canada or a return to responsible government as it had existed in 1933. "Of the two evils, choose the lesser," advised one writer to the *Daily News* who reluctantly supported the Canadian option. An anti-confederate writing from Grand Falls said, "We're quite capable of taking care of ourselves. To join with Canada, Never!"

In small communities like Norris Arm near Grand Falls the debate over the future took place in lumber camps during the week and at kitchen parties on the weekends. Along the northeast coast at Long Island in Notre Dame Bay a group of men gathered at the Orange Lodge to formally debate a return to responsible government versus a continuation of colonial status. Two women crashed the gathering, loudly demanding that confederation with Canada also be discussed. Farther along the coast at St. Anthony a straw vote was taken at a public meeting in May 1946. Confederation won that contest with responsible government garnering the support of just six out of the 300 residents at the meeting. Soon a national assembly would convene and the voices on all sides would get much louder.

Across the Atlantic the British public, exhausted by the war, had voted for change in the July 1945 election. The Conservatives, led by Winston Churchill, were ousted and Clement Atlee's Labour Party won by a landslide. Almost immediately the new government, which faced a crippling war debt, announced a radical new policy to rid itself of its overseas colonies. By January of 1946 the impact was felt in Newfoundland.

Walwyn received word in early January 1946 that he would be replaced. With barely two weeks to vacate Government House, which they had occupied for 10 years, the Walwyns began their round of ceremonial goodbyes.

Displaying a surprising petulance, Walwyn fired one last shot across the bow of those he perceived as his critics in St. John's. In a lengthy speech to a combined meeting of the Board of Trade and the Rotary Club, held in the ballroom of the Newfoundland Hotel on January 10, he enumerated a long list of his administration's achievements. The governor concluded by advising the press—the two daily newspapers in the city—to be more constructive, "not always so destructive." The editors of the papers, who had fancied themselves to be Walwyn's cheerleaders, thought the governor bitter and contemptuous. They were peeved and took exception to the remarks in their columns next day.

The self-styled "captain of the ship" left Government House at precisely 12:10 p.m. on January 17, 1946. The *Evening Telegram*, quoting from the official press statement, reported that the vice-regal party included His Excellency and Lady Walwyn, Chief Justice and Mrs. Emerson, and the commissioners and their wives. A cavalcade of four vehicles escorted by mounted policemen followed a route down Cochrane Street, along Duckworth Street, down Prescott Street, and west along Water Street past the Supreme Court Building to the railway station. As a crowd of 200 well-wishers sang "Auld Lang Syne," the Walwyns boarded their special railway coach, the *Terra Nova*, and departed for Stephenville. At Harmon Field they boarded an American military flight home.

Four days after the Walwyns' departure, the Labour government in London announced Walwyn's replacement. To everyone's surprise—especially those in the upper crust of St. John's society—Prime Minister Clement Atlee had not chosen an old Navy man with colonial experience. "For the first time in history," the BBC reported, "a working man was chosen for high office overseas."

Sir Gordon Macdonald was born on May 27, 1888, in Gwaenyscor, a quaint village nestled in the idyllic landscape of North Wales. Soon after his birth his family moved to the coal country of Lancashire and there he attended elementary school in the village of Stubshaw Cross. At the age of 13, Gordon followed his father and two brothers into the coal mines and started work as a pit boy. The family struggled after the father's death in 1903 and often sought relief from the Guardians of the Poor, the modern equivalent of a welfare agency.

During a debate in the House of Lords in 1950, Macdonald (now Lord Macdonald of Gwaenyscor) referred to these early experiences: "I, along with my fellow miners, left my home at five a.m. I spent over ten hours in the bowels of the earth and returned home at five p.m." After 54 hours a week of backbreaking labour he was rewarded with the paltry wage of a golden half-sovereign (about $20 in 2016 Canadian currency): "I clutched it and ran home with it until it nearly made a hole in the palm of my hand. I handed it to my mother, and she, in return gave me my pocket money, a silver three penny bit."

Such humble beginnings and the harsh conditions of the coal mines turned Macdonald into a champion of the working man. In his 20s he became a labour leader in the Lancashire and Cheshire Miners Federation and a driving force in the development of the Co-op Society of Lancashire. He was a clear thinker and a plain talker. In 1929, at age 40, he ran for election to parliament and became Labour member for Ince in Lancashire.

Macdonald survived the Labour setbacks of the Great Depression in the 1930s and became instrumental in focusing the social agenda of his party. As chair of committees in the House of Commons, he moved his party forward on issues like pensions, worker safety, corporal punishment in prisons, and the death penalty. During the war he served in a different role as a regional manager for Lancashire, Cheshire, and North Wales in the Ministry of Fuel and Power. For his distinguished service he received a knighthood in 1946.

At home in the coal country of Lancashire, Macdonald was widely admired for his speaking ability, a quality which his relatives say stemmed from his Welsh roots. His silver tongue made him a star speaker from church pulpits, in union halls, and on political platforms.

Macdonald arrived in Newfoundland to great fanfare on the afternoon of May 3, 1946. The justices of the Supreme Court, Mayor Carnell, the commissioners and their wives, and service heads of the American and Canadian forces greeted the new governor as he emerged from HMS *Fort Townshend* at the American military dock in the east end of St. John's Harbour. Governor Macdonald's party included Lady Macdonald, his daughter Glenys and his son Kenneth, who would be his father's private secretary.

That same afternoon Chief Justice Emerson administered the Oath of Allegiance to Office and Newfoundland's last British governor officially took charge. By the time of his departure three years later, life in Britain's oldest colony had undergone a seismic shift.

Much to the chagrin of society leaders in St. John's, Macdonald soon let it be known that the endless round of cocktail parties which had characterized Walwyn's time in office was not his style. In the city, news quickly spread—helped along by his son—that the new governor was a non-drinker, a non-smoker, and a deeply religious man.

From the beginning of his term Macdonald took an unusual approach to carrying out his official duties. "How could I best find out about my new job? Would I stay in Government House and ask the various representatives to come and see me and tell me about their troubles … throughout the country?" asked Macdonald. In short order he announced his intention to get out of the city at every opportunity and visit the small communities along the coast of the island and Labrador.

On the Newfoundland Express he made station stops in Lewisporte, Norris Arm, and Bishop's Falls. Ahead were visits to Grand Falls, Springdale, Twillingate, Little Bay Islands, Battle Harbour, and numerous other small outports up and down the coastline.

In the summer of 1947, Macdonald's tour along the Newfoundland and Labrador coast was made considerably easier by the presence of HMS *Padstow Bay*, a British Royal Navy frigate on a goodwill mission to North America. The speedy frigate enabled him to visit 12 communities in 12 days, from Fogo to Hopedale in northern Labrador and back to Corner Brook on the west coast. He preferred to travel, however, in small vessels like the hospital boat *Bonnie Nell* so that people were not intimidated by the arrival of this "bigshot" from the government in St. John's.

In Twillingate he taught a Sunday School class in the morning and delivered a frank sermon in the evening at St. Peter's Anglican Church. At Little Bay Islands he offered the blessing before sitting down to a community feast in his honour. He listened carefully as men spoke of living hand to mouth in small communities, without access to a hospital and without proper schooling for their children. He sought the views of women and reminded them that they too must be leaders in the debate over the future of their country. In every speech he called for 100 per cent turnout at the polls in the referendum set for June 3, 1948.

A reporter for the *Atlantic Guardian* interviewed the governor in the fall of 1947 and found him open and informal. Macdonald gave him a frank assessment of Newfoundland society. He found people in the outports friendly and intelligent and ready to give him their opinion on the state of the nation. He was disturbed, however, by their widespread poverty and poor health. He wondered if it would ever be possible to provide the services that people desperately needed in these small isolated communities.

The outport people called him "the governor of the poor." His impact was immediate and far-reaching. During his official visit to Twillingate, one resident thanked Macdonald and assured him that his interest in the working man had inspired people and awakened their confidence that better days lay ahead. By the end of 1947 he had become the most travelled governor Newfoundland had ever had.

During his visit to Norris Arm in the summer of 1947 the whole community turned out to greet him at the railway station. Among the crowd was a young man named Alfred Beaton. His fate would soon be intertwined with that of Sir Gordon.

Six

Don't shed any tears for me tonight.
—Alfred Beaton

The community of Norris Arm developed on an ancient flood plain of the Exploits River, a flat sandy strip of land hemmed in to the north by an arm of the Atlantic and to the south by a band of low hills. Nearby, the great river flows into the Bay of Exploits, its energy spent, after its long journey from the interior of Newfoundland. For the early settlers who came here after 1850 the river offered easy access to the rich hunting grounds used by Aboriginal people of an earlier time.

Royal Navy officer and explorer Captain David Buchan visited the area in the fall of 1810 in an unsuccessful bid to establish communication with the elusive Beothuk tribe. He tried again in the winter of 1820, attempting to make peaceful contact by returning a captive young Beothuk woman, Demasduit, to her people. Demasduit had been violently abducted by white settlers less than a year earlier and held at Twillingate. Unfortunately, Demasduit died of tuberculosis on board Buchan's sloop HMS *Grasshopper* a few days before the goodwill expedition had scheduled its departure inland and peace initiative was abandoned. HMS *Grasshopper* remained anchored and frozen in the ice just across the inlet from Norris Arm for the rest of the winter.

It was not until the 1890s that a large number of settlers arrived in Norris Arm from outlying communities along the northeast coast. Over the next 30 years newcomers flocked to this sheltered place. The Elliots arrived from Fogo and the Budgells from the Exploits Island. The Beatons moved in from Upper Sandy Point and the Dwyers from Holyrood. Families resettled from St. John's, Stephenville, and Bonavista, and to break the pattern, several families arrived from Lebanon on the shores of the Mediterranean Sea. They came because of the railway and opportunities for jobs and businesses.

As the crow flies, Norris Arm sat little more than halfway between the larger and better known towns of Lewisporte and Bishop's Falls. On the Newfoundland Express, or the Newfie Bullet, workers from Norris Arm could reach flourishing towns like Gander with its busy airport and Grand Falls with its large paper mill in a few hours. In the decade before Confederation, families like the Beatons, the Dwyers, and the Elliots did not have to travel far to find jobs.

The Saunders & Howell Company ran a large sawmill operation in the community, producing building supplies for rapidly expanding centres like Grand Falls and Corner Brook. The mill employed as many as 60 workers, not including the dozens of lumbermen needed to feed the mill from the rich stands of timber located inland from the community. The company owned the largest retail store as well, and housed many of their employees in a company-sponsored housing development known as the Range.

In December 1945, Ranger Clarence Dwyer, Norris Arm's police officer, reported that 105 men were employed by Saunders & Howell: "A large crowd was also employed by the A.N.D. Company at Great Rattling Brook, others are still employed at Gander ... All the men at this place are earning large wages."

With all that money flowing into Norris Arm, Dwyer worried unnecessarily, it seemed, about trouble: "despite the greatest amount of liquor ever known arriving from St. John's this Christmas season, I did not see one man drunk or so drunk that he caused any trouble." Dwyer attended every social event and every dance as a warning to potential troublemakers. All was quiet. "The reason for the quietness was the fact that [he] was up against three of the known hard cases here and they came off second best ..."

The Commission of Government had established the rural police force known as the Newfoundland Rangers in 1935. At a training base established in Whitbourne, 75 kilometres outside of St. John's, the recruits trained under the direction of Sergeant-Major Anderton, on loan from the Royal Canadian Mounted Police. The Rangers met the exacting standards of that world-famous police force and in short order acquired some of the mystique of the Mounties.

The Rangers dressed in distinctive khaki uniforms with a brown stripe down the trouser leg. They were required to carry a .38 calibre pistol at all times, but few did. In the 15 years of the force's history, not one shot was fired in the line of duty. By the time they were absorbed by the RCMP in 1950, stories of the Rangers' sense of adventure, endurance, and bravery were the stuff of legend.

The Rangers patrolled the rugged interior and the coastal stretches of Newfoundland and Labrador. Along the Gander River they watched for wildlife poachers operating in the backcountry; on the west coast, for American herring seiners operating inside territorial waters; and along the south coast, for schooners running under full sail with their cargoes of contraband rum from the French islands of St. Pierre and Miquelon.

But the Rangers were more than peace officers. As they patrolled the small outport communities during the Depression years, they were met with the hollow-eyed stares of hungry children and the pleas of desperate mothers trying to ward off starvation on 6 cents a day. Only the most critical cases qualified for relief under the hard-nosed policy of the Commission of Government.

In the absence of doctors and nurses the Rangers improvised. Using knowledge from basic first-aid training received in Whitbourne, they stitched wounds with cotton thread, set broken bones with plaster tape, and extracted teeth using a codeine pill as a painkiller.

Within a decade after 1935 the Rangers had established their presence at about 60 communities on the island and in Labrador. The words "the Ranger is coming" were enough not only to deter wrongdoing but also to bring hope to families in need.

At the Norris Arm detachment in 1946, Ranger Dwyer supervised road repair projects, issued game licences, and enforced forestry regulations. In 1947, when Ranger Jacobs replaced Dwyer he dispensed cocoamalt and cod liver oil to malnourished children and investigated several cases of non-attendance at school. In a brief downturn in the local economy that year it became necessary to issue poor relief to 42 people.

Prosperity returned to the busy community near the mouth of the Exploits in 1948. "When all the men return to this community from Glenwood, Gander and other places," reported Jacobs, "they bring extra money to improve the place as these people are all repairing or painting their houses or building new ones." Many young women found work in the big stores in Grand Falls or as servant girls to well-off families in Botwood and Bishop's Falls. Everyone felt hopeful about the future.

But there was a dark undercurrent of trouble brewing in Norris Arm that spring. Gossip had begun to spread during the winter that all was not well in Frank Beaton's family. Everyone in town knew that the Beaton family had gone through a rough patch since the tragic death of Frank's wife, Mary, in 1946. Most people tried to be understanding.

Alfred, the oldest son, worked with his father in the lumber camps. Men working in the camps brought back stories that the young man was a loner, acted strangely, and refused to have anything to do with the other men. On weekends, 18-year-old Alfred picked fights in town, especially when he was drinking. His girlfriend, Margaret Stuckless, kept her distance when she knew he'd been "into the sauce."

Fifty-year-old Ernest Beaton, Alfred's uncle, experienced first-hand his nephew's blind rage and aggression. Ernest was relaxing at home on St. Patrick's in March 1948 when his brother, Frank, came by for a late-night visit. The five children and his wife, Alice, were sleeping. Over a few drinks at the kitchen table the two men listened to the late news on the radio and argued amiably over how they would vote in the June referendum.

"Alfred Beaton, my nephew, came in the door just after midnight," said Ernest. "I could tell by looking at him, he had liquor in. He took out a bottle with between three and four inches of rum in it." He offered his father and uncle a drink. They poured themselves a shot from Alfred's bottle and continued with their conversation.

Alfred sat in brooding silence on the couch. Suddenly he broke in, "Don't listen to him Uncle Ern, he doesn't know what he's talking about."

The two older men tried to ignore the remark but their easy conversation was now replaced by an awkward silence in the kitchen. Suddenly Alfred leapt to his feet and headed outside, slamming the door angrily. An instant later he was back without his cap and coat challenging his father to fight and ordering him from the house.

Ernest said, "Hold on a minute, Alf, you can't do that. You can't drive anyone out of my house."

Alfred ignored his uncle and hovered angrily over his father. "Just come outside. We're going to have it out."

Frank tried to calm his son down but eventually got up and followed Alfred out the door. Ernest grabbed his coat and followed, but by the time he was outside, father and son were clenched and rolling on the ground. Ernest was able to separate the two and held Alfred by the arm as he pulled him to his feet. He pushed his brother away at the same time and steered Alfred toward the railway track in the direction of his home.

Alfred said, "Uncle, let me go. I got to get him."

"No, Alf," replied Ernest, "you're not doing anything of the kind tonight. Go home now and be a good boy."

Despite Ernest's best efforts to calm his nephew down, Alfred was determined to renew his attack on his father. He reached into his pocket and pulled out a pocket knife.

"Look, Uncle," he said, "I'm using this tonight."

The fight took a frightening turn as Alfred waved the knife in his uncle's face. Ernest feared for his own safety and tried to convince Alfred to give up the knife.

Alfred suddenly pulled loose from his uncle and was on his father again, punching and cursing. Ernest grabbed Alfred again, threw him to the ground, and pinned him by the neck while he searched him for the knife. He found the weapon in Alfred's pocket and pulled him roughly to his feet.

"Go for the Ranger. Go for the Ranger," Ernest shouted to his brother.

Frank ran and, when he was a safe distance down the track, Ernest released Alfred and calmly told him to go home.

Alfred responded with a chilling threat, "I'm going to get a gun."

Ernest went back inside, convinced that more trouble was brewing. He stood by the window for half an hour looking up the road for any sign of Alfred's return. Finally, he decided the threat had passed, and he went to bed.

At 2 a.m. Frank and Ranger Ledrew showed up at the door. Ernest got out of bed and talked to the two men. They decided it would be safer for Frank to stay the night at his brother's house.

Frank Beaton provided a detailed statement to Ledrew the next morning of his son's hair-trigger temper. "He has threatened to get me twice now and I believe he means to kill me with some weapon at any time he becomes provoked," he told Ledrew. Frank stressed that he needed help in dealing with his son before it was too late. "I am in mortal fear of my son, Alfred, and want whatever protection the law can provide," said Frank.

Over the coming months other incidents came to light. On August 2, 1948, Richard Lacey, a 67-year-old resident of Norris Arm came to see the temporary police officer in town, Ranger Flight. Lacey told Flight he had twice been assaulted by Alfred Beaton. On Sunday night, July 18, Beaton had attacked him for no reason when the two met near the Saunders & Howell store. Lacey fought back, and Alfred backed off. Now something more sinister had taken place which made him fear for his life.

Lacey told Flight that around midnight on July 18 he decided to go down to the government wharf to check on his small passenger boat because the tide was extremely low. As he walked between the post office and the railway station, Beaton had emerged from the shadows and struck him on the head with a piece of wood. It was a senseless attack and Beaton had simply said, "Nobody will be a witness to what's going on tonight."

Beaton struck just once, then turned and ran toward the railway station. Lacey, infuriated but still determined to check his boat, ran back to his home to get something to protect himself. This time on the way to the wharf there was no sign of the attacker. Lacey threw away the stick he carried as he turned for home, confident that nothing else would happen.

As Lacey neared his home, he heard footsteps behind him and, without warning, Beaton struck again. A blow to the head knocked Lacey to the ground. His screams for help brought Jim Pardy, a neighbour, out of his house. Pardy shouted at the attacker and Beaton fled into the darkness.

Despite the violent incident, Flight did not charge Beaton for the assault on Richard Lacey, a decision which only added to growing tension in the town.

In the fall of 1948, an Indian summer stretched well into October along the northeast coast and in central Newfoundland. On the hills west of Norris Arm the brilliant reds and mottled orange of the Newfoundland maple and silver birch broke the monotony of the thick evergreen forest. Saturday, October 23, brought a peculiar stillness to the community, an eerie calm that sometimes came at that time of year. Only the occasional babble of children's voices in the morning air broke the oppressive silence.

The railway strike, which had started on October 11, also silenced the comforting rumble of the freight trains rolling slowly through the community at night. At the station in the centre of the community a few people still gathered late each afternoon in the vain hope they might hear the distant moan of the Newfoundland Express en route to St. John's. It was quiet, too quiet.

At the railway station, agent Michael Hogan kept a watchful eye on the Newfoundland Railway property. He tried to keep busy by catching up on paperwork, only too well aware of the rising frustration of people working in Gander, Grand Falls, and Glenwood who had no transportation to and from their jobs. The day before, he learned that some men had walked the 40 miles along the track from Gander to spend a few days at home with their families.

The new Ranger, Bruce Gillingham, who arrived in September, was also concerned about the impact of the rail strike on the community. Supplies of fresh food were noticeably diminishing in the stores and essentials like flour and sugar would run out unless the dispute was settled soon. To him fell the job of monitoring the needs of seniors and poor families as well as attending to his police duties. On the positive side, he thought, weekends were quieter without the regular shipments of alcohol arriving with travellers from Grand Falls and Gander.

Irven Manual, who lived with his parents, Herbert and Joanna, took advantage of the good weather to finish work on a new barn and was happy to have his cousin, Alfred Beaton, arrive in the early afternoon to help out. To fortify themselves against the work ahead, they decided to sample Irven's new batch of molasses beer, still unfinished and yeasty, but already with a bit of a kick. After five glasses each they went to work. Sometime between 5 and 5:30 p.m. they went back to the house and drank another three glasses each. Irven recalled that Alfred appeared to be sober when he left the house around 6 to return home for the evening meal.

Alfred's youngest sister, 15-year-old Marie, remembered her brother's returning home around 6 p.m. and sitting at the dinner table with her older sister, Margaret, and their young brother, Francis. In Marie's statement to police the next day she would say she knew that Alfred had been drinking when he came home, as he seemed to be a little drunk: "He did not stagger but I could see that he had been drinking."

In a statement to Gillingham on the same day, Margaret offered a similar picture. Alfred appeared to have been drinking when he came home. His face was flushed and he was quiet around the house. As soon as he finished his supper, he left the house and she did not see him again that night.

On the way back to Irven's place after dinner, Alfred visited another friend, who gave him a glass of homebrew. Around 7:30 p.m. he arrived at Irven's and they sat around drinking more homebrew while listening to the Doyle News Bulletin on the radio.

Around 9 p.m. they left to visit the Robinsons nearby, where a few other men, including Hallett Manuel, Irven's brother, were drinking. Irven recalled that Alfred drank three glasses of homebrew there while he himself was finishing one.

Over at the Exploits Inn, better known in the community as Michael Ryan's parlour, the night was still quiet. A small group including Margaret Stuckless, Ruby Elliot, Warrick Walker, and Johnny Stuckless were sitting at one of the tables when Jim Dwyer arrived around 9 p.m. Jim ordered a Moose Ale, sat down with the group, and struck up a conversation with Margaret. The two were still talking when Alfred Beaton and Irven Manuel arrived shortly after 9. The two stood by the counter and ordered a beer each. Everyone there clearly remembered the events that followed.

"When we got there," said Irven, "I saw Johnny Stuckless, his sister Margaret, and Jim Dwyer at a table. Alfred Beaton walked over to the table and he asked Margaret could he see her for a minute."

Jim Dwyer had courted Margaret until late 1947, but she had broken off their relationship when he started working at a new job in Gander. Margaret then began a relationship with Alfred. Dwyer's presence anywhere near Margaret did not sit well with Alfred. "If you go near Margaret again," he had warned Jim in one encounter, "I'll use my gun on you." Now Jim saw Alfred walking over to their table. Jim noticed a sheath with a knife handle showing on his belt.

Jim remembered Alfred's exact words. "Excuse me, Jim. Margaret, come outside, I want to see you."

Jim noticed nothing out of the ordinary in Alfred's tone. "Both Margaret Stuckless and Beaton went outside. I stayed and had a bottle of beer with my friends and about five minutes later I left to go home."

Ruby Elliot's recollections were much the same. "Alfred Beaton then came over to our table and said, 'Excuse me, Jim. Can I see you for a moment, Margaret, please?' The voice was in an ordinary tone, and he did not appear to be angry. I paid no attention to him."

Margaret's memories of the events coincided with those of the others. "Alfred Beaton came over to the table where I was and asked me to go outside. At the time I was talking to Jim Dwyer and Alfred said, 'Pardon me, Jim. Come out, Margaret, I want you.'"

Beaton's behaviour triggered no alarm bells for Margaret or her friends. "Alfred was wearing breeks, logans, grey socks, and had on a sweater, over which he had braces … I did not see anything out of the ordinary about him at this time."

When the couple stepped outside, events took a dramatic turn. "Who do you want, Jim or me?" demanded Alfred.

"I thought he was only fooling," said Margaret, "so I said, I'm not particular, either one of you will do."

It was then that Margaret realized that Alfred was deadly serious. "I'm going home," she said. She began to walk away but Alfred grabbed her roughly, jerked her around, and lashed out. Something smashed into her face just below the left eye.

A few minutes after Margaret and Alfred had gone outside, Jim Dwyer finished his beer and left Ryan's parlour to go home. He saw the couple struggling about 30 feet away and immediately sensed something was wrong. Beaton said, "Come here Jim, I want you." As he approached, Margaret screamed, "I'm stabbed, Jim."

The next instant Dwyer, too, was shocked by a powerful blow from some object in Alfred's hand. Confused and in a daze he ran for home. He heard Alfred's voice, close by. "You ran, didn't you? I'll get you." The other patrons, alerted by the screams outside, streamed from the parlour.

Ruby Elliot reached Margaret first. "Oh my God, Alf got me stabbed," she said to Ruby. Margaret put her hand up and felt a knife blade sticking in her face. Instinctively she pulled the blade out and threw it in the ditch. Her jacket was covered in blood.

Johnny Stuckless, Margaret's brother, was on the scene as well. He asked Ruby to take his sister home. Despite her pain Margaret insisted she could not go home because her mother would be frightened. Ruby decided to take Margaret to Mrs. Budgell's, where she knew she could get first aid.

Johnny ran to look for Gillingham. It was close to 9:30 p.m. The night of terror was just beginning.

Alfred's sister Marie was the first one to see her brother after the violent incident outside Michael Ryan's parlour. She was at home looking after her brother Francis, who was asleep, when Alfred stormed into the house a little after 9:30. He went straight to the bedroom, grabbed his father's 44.40 Winchester hunting rifle, gathered as many shells as he could find, and headed out the door. "I asked him where he was going with the gun," said Marie, "and he didn't say anything." Alfred left the house at 9:45 p.m. and within a few minutes she heard the first shots somewhere down the road.

When Alfred left home, he headed east on the main road, which ran parallel to the railway track. A waning three-quarter moon shone between scudding clouds. He broke the stillness with several shots from his 44.40. At the far end of the community to the west, Stan Langdon had just finished chopping up some firewood. To him the shots sounded muffled, "like someone dropping a pile of lumber."

Earnest Beaton's 15-year-old son, Leonard, had been visiting Maurice Macdonald's house listening to the "Ralph and Don" programme on VONF. When the programme finished at 9:30 p.m., he walked back home and asked his mother, Alice, to get him a snack. They had just sat down at the table when they heard the first shot. Both thought it must be the Ranger shooting dogs.

Leonard left his lunch unfinished and went out on the steps to check. Just up the road a dark figure approached and a voice asked, "Is that you, Uncle?"

"No, it's me," said Leonard, as he recognized the voice of his first cousin, Alfred.

Alfred asked him where his father was and Leonard told him he was up to Mary Flynn's playing cards.

"This is the night for him to be out here," said Alfred.

From the tone of Alfred's voice, Leonard thought his father might be in danger. He went inside but became more alarmed as gunfire again rang out just to the west. He suggested to his mother that they take the two younger children and try to reach the safety of Ambrose Saunders's home just up the road. As soon as they were outside, the lights of the Saunders house went out. They would have to find another way to safety.

Just down the main road on the other side of the tracks Jim Dwyer's mother cleaned the blood from her son's neck and bandaged the wound inflicted by Alfred. They too heard the sound of gunfire. Mrs. Dwyer locked the doors and turned out the kerosene lamps. The terrified family stayed well away from the windows and huddled on a daybed in the living room. A window shattered in the porch as four quick shots rang out. No one moved. A few minutes of silence, and they heard the next shot farther to the west. The gunman had moved on.

Alice Beaton and Leonard decided it was too dangerous to walk down the road to find safety with the Goodyears, who lived near the government seaplane hangar. Instead they cautiously led the two younger children to a rowboat on the shoreline and began rowing west toward the hangar. They landed in silence. Alice and the two younger boys reached the safety of the Goodyear home, but Leonard was determined to warn his father that his life might be in danger:

> I left Goodyear's to go to Mrs. Flynn's. I climbed through the fence between Goodyear's and Manuel's. I had to go up a grade. As I started away from the fence I heard someone say, "Okay son." As soon as he spoke to me he fired a gun and I saw the flame of the gun right in front of me. I did not recognize the voice but it was a man. When the shot was fired I felt my right arm being pulled back. I ran back then to Stan Goodyears; after I got in the house I heard shots and they seemed to come from the direction of the station.

It would be next morning before Leonard discovered just how close to death he had come.

Johanna Manuel, Alfred's aunt, who lived near the Goodyears, was startled by the rifle blast so close to her house. She jumped out of her chair, turned down the radio, and rushed outside to investigate:

I went to the gate by the front of the house. I saw a person by the side of the road. I didn't recognize the person at the time but he came towards me, and I said, "Who fired that shot?" He said, "I did." He came up near and I saw the person was Alfred Beaton ... I said, "Alf, my son, you are not allowed to have that gun tonight. Give me the gun and I'll take it in the house and you can have it first thing in the morning. He said, "No." And I said again, "give me the gun ..." He said, "No, not until I am finished with it." I didn't say anything else. He turned and walked east and said, "Don't shed any tears for me tonight."

Johanna noticed that Alfred spoke "real low." Otherwise she remembered him as being normal and "he did not appear angry."

Gillingham remained unaware of the trouble brewing at the east end of Norris Arm. He was visiting Mrs. Allan Poole when Norman Stuckless, Margaret's younger brother, burst in just before 10 p.m. and informed him that Margaret had been stabbed in front of the Exploits Inn. Gillingham followed the young man to Elsie Budgell's house, where Margaret lay on a couch in shock. He saw a gash about 1 inch long under Margaret's left eye. He gave first-aid instructions and told them he would try to call a doctor from Botwood.

Gillingham's first task was to find Beaton and make an arrest. Along with John Stuckless, who had arrived at Budgell's, he headed east down the main road toward Frank Beaton's home.

"We left Mrs. Budgell's and went down the lane which is known as Budgell's Lane to the main road," said Gillingham, "and just as we turned east I heard William Beason a short distance from us, who came to me and informed me that there was shooting down east and that while he was near the front steps of Gerald Ryan's parlour a bullet had whizzed past his head." Gillingham realized he was facing a dangerous situation and would need to be armed.

Gillingham, Stuckless, and Beason ran first to Edgar Perry's home, where Gillingham borrowed a 44.40 Winchester rifle and six cartridges.

They then hurried to Brinston's, Gillingham's boarding house, where he collected his .38 revolver. He loaded both weapons. As they were leaving Brinston's, they noticed a figure hurrying west in the shadows on the other side of the road. Gillingham was suspicious but issued no challenge. The shooting up to this point seemed to be confined to the east end of the community.

The three men walked cautiously eastward down the railway track from Brinston's to Ryan's, where the stabbing had taken place. They had gone no more than 500 yards when a shot rang out behind them. Gillingham realized the figure he had seen moments earlier must have been the gunman.

Sam Elliot heard the same shot. He had been at home all night listening to the Grand Ole Opry on the radio. The shot seemed to come from the west, quite close to his home on Range Road. He ran outside and stood in the gateway. After a minute he slowly walked along Range Road in the direction of the shot.

> I walked about ten feet when I saw the form of a man about twenty-five feet to the west of me. A voice said, "stick 'em up," and I jumped back behind my own gate. I crouched down and ran towards my house. Before I got there I heard a shot … I recognized the voice as that of Alfred Beaton. I went in the house and told my wife to keep the children away from the windows as I was afraid the bullets would come through.

The gunman had now made his way over half a mile from the east end of the community along the main road and had now entered the western end of the Range. Twenty families occupied homes on either side of the main road running through this section of the community. A gunman on the loose in this area posed a serious threat.

Gillingham and his two companions turned around and ran in the direction of the gunfire. When they reached the corner of the Saunders & Howell store, another shot broke the evening quiet.

After hearing this second shot I ran through a part meadow and part lane just east of the store … towards the corner of a fence near a new house being built by Rowsell at the eastern end of the road running through the Range … Beason and Stuckless were just behind me. When I got to about twelve feet from the corner of the fence I stopped and passed over the rifle to John Stuckless and informed him that I was going on but in the event that I was shot I asked him to try to get the person that shot me. I then told them to take cover behind a big rock which was there.

Gillingham moved forward searching the darkness for any sign of movement.

As word spread about the stabbing outside the Exploits Inn, people began to gather at the home of Mrs. Budgell, where Margaret was being treated. Ruby Elliot had stayed on after she had brought Margaret to the home around 9:30 p.m. Ten minutes later, Annie Stuckless, Margaret's mother, arrived. Her son had informed her that his sister had been injured. She stayed to console her daughter and to help Mrs. Budgell. The women heard the sound of gunfire to the east and shortly afterward, several shots to the west of the house. They became more and more apprehensive as the evening wore on. "Everyone was very upset," recalled Ruby.

Three hundred yards east of Mrs. Budgell's, her daughter, Dorothea, anxiously waited for her husband, Hallett Manuel, to return home from Robinson's. Her two young boys had been asleep for several hours and showed no signs of awakening despite the sounds of gunfire in the community. Her husband finally came home around 10:20 p.m. with news about some unusual activity at her mother's house.

Hallett had heard the first shots and, like many others in the community, thought little of it at first, but as the gunfire continued, he became worried. He wondered if someone been injured and taken to Mrs. Budgell's. After finding a neighbour to look after the two children, they decided to go down to find out what was happening. "It was about 10:30," recalled Hallett, "we left our house and went to the house of my wife's mother, Mrs. Elsie Budgell. When we got to my mother-in-law's we saw

Margaret Stuckless there lying on a couch with her eye bandaged."

Hallett and Dorothea stayed for more than half an hour with her mother, but when several more shots rang out in the Range area they became uneasy about the children and decided to return home. Ruby and Annie left with them. They went out the back door and turned right onto Range Road. They had gone no more than 20 steps when a deafening rifle blast sent the group into a panic.

Gillingham was about to turn the corner of the fence and walk west along Range Road when he saw a dark figure approaching. The figure was pointing an object to the west, away from Gillingham. As he recalled:

> at that moment flame and a report came from the object and I knew it was a gun. The man was standing a little to the left of the centre of the road … and about thirty feet from the house of Stan Langdon … and about one hundred feet from where I was at the time. He was holding the rifle at shoulder level pointing west.

There was a bright moon moving in and out of scattered cloud, "not a real dark night," recalled Gillingham, who could clearly see the actions of the gunman.

> After the flash of the gun I saw this person turn and start to run in my direction. I turned back around the corner of the fence and saw him cross the road to the right side, the side that I was on…. When some thirteen feet from me he knelt down facing west with the rifle in a kneeling shooting position … with his back to me. I rounded the corner of the fence and made for the man, and when crossing a large stone I kicked a tin can. The man saw me and turned and when a matter of one or two feet from the man he fired at me. The bullet, from the direction of the flame, I took to go between my arm and my right side. When I jumped on the man the gun wedged between my right arm and side.

But Gillingham now had a problem; there was intense pain in his elbow and his right arm had gone numb. Thinking he had been shot he called to Beason and Stuckless. The three men overpowered the gunman and Gillingham soon discovered that in tackling him he had knocked his elbow on the fence. "I took the rifle from the man," said Gillingham. "It was a 44.40 Winchester. I recognized the man as Alfred Beaton."

Just up the road in the direction of Beaton's previous shot, a far more serious incident was unfolding. Hallett Manuel described the scene:

> We went about six yards when I heard a shot. At this time my wife, myself and Ruby Elliot were together. My wife was in the centre, I was to the right of her with my left arm around her waist and Ruby Elliot was on the left of my wife close to her. Mrs. Stuckless was a few feet ahead of us, walking to the left of my wife. The shot appeared to come from the east but I did not turn around and I would say it was about one hundred feet away. When the shot was fired my wife fell back in my arms, and I laid her on the ground and kept her head up … I then felt the back part of her coat getting wet, the part around her shoulders. I then realized she had been hit.

With the loud report of the gun so close, both Ruby Elliot and Annie Stuckless instinctively ran for the cover of Stan Langdon's house a short distance away. When Ruby reached the Langdon deck, she looked back and saw Dorothea Manuel on the ground with her husband kneeling beside her. "I asked Mr. Manuel what was the matter," said Ruby, "and he said Dot was shot. I then ran back and went into Mrs. Budgell's and told her."

When Hallett realized that Dorothea was critically injured, he shouted for help. In his statement to the preliminary inquiry at Grand Falls on December 3, he described the scene: "A minute or so afterwards Gilbert and Allan Purchase came along, lifted my wife off the ground and brought her into her mother's house, Mrs. Elsie Budgell. She was then unconscious and I went into the house also. My wife died shortly after."

In the darkness a few hundred yards to the east, Beaton was in a rage as he was held down by Beason and Stuckless. As Gillingham struggled to handcuff his prisoner, he was unaware of the tragedy unfolding down the road. The scuffle with Beaton drowned out any sound coming from that direction, and a dip in the road in front of the Langdon home obscured the movements of people assisting the fatally wounded woman.

Gillingham pulled Beaton to his feet and informed him that he was arrested for the stabbing of Margaret Stuckless. He had to get his prisoner to the jail in Botwood, a short boat trip away. They set off first for the railway station, where he deposited the rifles with station agent Michael Hogan and asked that the firearms be kept in a secure location until he returned.

Arthur Whitt, who operated one of two passenger-boat services to Botwood, agreed to make the night trip across the inlet with the four men. John Stuckless offered his account of Beaton's behaviour as they waited for the boat:

> From the time of Beaton's arrest and the time we brought him to the government wharf, he did not say anything but while on the wharf he wanted to see me alone and he told me to tell my sister he was sorry for what he had done. He did not say anything more at any time. Beason and myself went with the Ranger and the accused to Botwood where he was brought to the police station.

The group arrived at the police station in Botwood at midnight and were met by Sergeant Gosling and Constable Bennett of the Newfoundland Constabulary. Bennett searched the prisoner and took him to a cell.

With Beaton behind bars, Gillingham contacted Dr. Gerald Smith and asked him to return with him to Norris Arm to tend to Margaret Stuckless. The two constabulary officers also agreed to go along and assist with the investigation.

At 12:20 a.m. they left Botwood for what they thought would be an uneventful trip back to Norris Arm. Ten minutes later, in mid-channel, another boat signalled them in the darkness. "We saw a boat approaching," said Gillingham. "They were using a flashlight, and we went towards the boat which was driven by Richard Lacey, when we were informed that Mrs. Hallett Manuel had been shot and was presumed to be dead."

Gillingham realized he was now dealing with a murder as well as a case of aggravated assault.

The officers also realized at that moment that a dangerous prisoner had been left unguarded in a cell at the Botwood jail. Gosling instructed Constable Bennett to return in Lacey's boat and mount careful watch on Beaton. A long night and a difficult investigation awaited Gillingham when he arrived back in Norris Arm at 1 a.m., Sunday, October 24, with Smith and Gosling.

Gosling and Smith proceeded directly to Mrs. Budgell's home. Gillingham went to the railway station to retrieve the weapons he had left in the care of Hogan earlier that night. Beaton's 44.40 still had one round of ammunition in the magazine and an empty cartridge in the breech. When Gillingham arrived at the Budgell home, many of the neighbours had gathered in shocked disbelief outside. Some were softly weeping. Inside he found Margaret Stuckless lying on a couch with her left eye bandaged. In another room he saw the body of Dorothea Manuel. Dr. Smith confirmed that she was dead.

Nobody in Norris Arm slept much during the night. The hours of terror during which a gunman stalked the darkened roads, firing indiscriminately, had traumatized the community. At daylight next morning people began to take stock and share stories of narrow escapes.

Over at Ernest Beaton's home, Leonard woke after a restless sleep and began dressing in the clothes he had worn the night before. He noticed two holes in the right sleeve of his blue shirt, a hole in the right sleeve of his underwear just above the cuff, and two holes in the right sleeve of his windbreaker.

Three bullets had torn through the walls of Jim Dwyer's home 2 or 3 feet above floor level as he, his father, and his mother had cowered in the darkness. Another had smashed through the window in their porch. All the slugs were recovered during the investigation.

A bullet had gone through Edgar Perry's house just a few feet above floor level. Beaton was known to have a strong dislike for the Perry family. Another shot had hit the fence in the exact spot where Perry was in the habit of standing in the evenings while smoking his pipe.

Two others had ripped through Stan Goodyear's home while the family huddled in a corner of the kitchen. William Beason had missed death by inches as a bullet had whizzed by his head as he chatted with two girls on the steps of Gerald Ryan's parlour.

At the Botwood jail, Beaton stayed awake in his cell under the watchful eye of Constable Bennett, who conducted a check every 20 minutes. At 3 a.m., he observed the prisoner removing his boots and, while doing so, Beaton gave him a rifle shell which had been missed in the earlier search. Between 4 and 5 a.m., as Bennett conducted another check, Beaton wanted to talk. "It's an awful thing I've done tonight," he said. Beaton cautioned him:

> At the office I informed him that he would likely be charged with the unlawful killing of a human being named Dorothea Manuel, and also assaulting one Margaret Stuckless, with a dangerous weapon causing her grievous bodily injury. I told him he was not bound to say anything or make any statement, but anything he would now say would be taken down in writing and may be used as evidence. He then started to tell me what happened …

The two sat across from each other and Beaton talked uninterrupted about what had happened during the previous night:

> Last night at about nine p.m. or nine-thirty p.m., I went into Ryan's Beer Parlour and my girl, Margaret Stuckless, was sitting there with another fellow, Jim Dwyer. I asked her out to the door and she came out to the door and I asked her to talk to me and she said, "I'm not talking to you." She come out of the beer parlour and wanted to go home and I walked from the store down to the road with her and I asked her what was wrong and she wouldn't tell me. I struck her with the knife that I had on my belt. I left her then and went home and got the rifle and went up the road and I fired five or six shots out of the rifle. The most of them I fired up in the air. I knowed nothing until when I was going across the range when "buddy,"

the Ranger, caught me and brought me to the police station in Botwood and waited for you fellows to come.

Alfred Beaton signed his statement at 5:40 a.m. on Sunday morning and was escorted back to his cell.

At 10:05 a.m., a float plane carrying Capt. Glendenning from Ranger headquarters in Whitbourne landed on the inlet at Norris Arm. The former banker-turned-police officer had earned a reputation as a meticulous detective, well known throughout Newfoundland and in Labrador. His detailed investigation over the next four days left nothing to chance.

With the assistance of Gillingham, Glendenning carefully mapped Beaton's rampage through the community. They recovered bullets from the interior walls of homes, photographed crime scenes, interviewed witnesses, and secured pieces of evidence such as the clothing of young Leonard Beaton.

Dr. Sutherland, the chief surgeon at the Botwood hospital, conducted a post-mortem on the body of the shooting victim on October 24 in the presence of Glendenning and Smith. They found that the high velocity bullet had entered the victim's back just below the shoulder blade to the left of the spine, severing the pulmonary artery and vein. They determined the cause of death to be internal bleeding complicated by severe shock.

On October 25, Beaton appeared in front of Magistrate B.J. Abbott in Grand Falls. Abbott ordered that the prisoner be held on remand in the Grand Falls jail for a preliminary hearing beginning on December 3, 1948.

Newspapers across the island carried front-page headlines on the slaying in central Newfoundland on October 25. The Doyle Bulletin on the Broadcasting Corporation of Newfoundland (BCN) network spread the grim news from Norris Arm to households all over the island on its Monday night broadcast. Lead stories emphasized the young age of the alleged murderer as well as the narrow escape of Gillingham when fired upon while in pursuit of the accused.

The *Twillingate Sun* carried the story on October 30. Details were scanty but that did not deter the editor from describing the action in the style of a good western. In this embellished version, four women came upon the gunman on a dark road and one was shot: "Ranger Gillingham was notified by the other three women who rushed back to the village to secure help. After an exciting chase during which he was fired upon by Beaton … the Ranger took him into custody."

The weekly *Grand Falls Advertiser* also carried the story on October 30. "Fatal Shooting Follows Stabbing at Norris Arm," screamed its banner headline. "Dorothea Manuel Dies and Margaret Stuckless Hospitalized after Saturday Night Fracas." The sensational story grabbed public attention and for several days it deflected worry over the impact of the railway walkout.

The strike, which had now dragged on for two weeks, showed no signs of a settlement. Rail and coastal boat traffic, the lifeline of communities outside St. John's, lay idle. In centres like Grand Falls, traffic came to a standstill because of gas shortages and there was a real danger that the paper mill would cease operations. The travel disruptions also upset the Central district court schedule in Grand Falls.

A sense of panic began to set in along the coast where families began to worry about their supplies of flour, canned milk, salt beef, and the other items which kept starvation at bay in the cold winter months. "There is no doubt that tempers are getting badly frayed," warned the *Twillingate Sun* on November 6, "and desperate men do desperate things."

Alarmed residents flooded newspaper offices with letters to the editor. "How can the government allow 2800 railway workers to hold 320,000 people hostage?" wrote one irate citizen of Twillingate. Petitions from across the colony implored Governor Macdonald to intervene.

The deepening gloom of the strike further dampened spirits in Norris Arm where the community had not recovered from the tragic death of one of its own. A young mother with two sons had been taken from them; emotions were raw and vengeance plagued the minds of some. Guy Fawkes Night, November 5, a highly anticipated event in Newfoundland, fell on a Friday, but no one had an appetite for bonfires or celebration.

On November 12, the strike ended and the rail unions accepted a final offer from the government. On Friday, November 13, the familiar rumble of rolling stock and the moan of the passenger express returned across the island.

With the return of passenger service, the court in Grand Falls could now move ahead with plans for the preliminary inquiry to determine if there was sufficient evidence to commit Alfred Beaton to trial at the Supreme Court of Newfoundland in St. John's. Examination of witnesses began at the Grand Falls courthouse in front of Magistrate Abbott. The Director of Public Prosecutions, H.P. Carter, who had been present at the Spratt trial in 1942, arrived by train from St. John's to represent the crown.

Twenty-four witnesses, mostly residents of Norris Arm, gave evidence at the inquiry. These included Marie Beaton, sister of the accused; Hallett Manuel, the grieving husband of the victim; Margaret Stuckless, the stabbing victim; and young Leonard Beaton, who had experienced a narrow escape during the night of terror in October.

Alfred Beaton was not represented by counsel and sat quietly throughout the proceedings breaking his silence only when the final witness, his cousin, Irven Manuel, took the stand. Beaton simply wanted to know how many glasses of beer he had drunk at Irven's house before and after tea on October 23. "About five glasses before tea," replied Irven, "and one glass after tea." The issue of how much beer Alfred consumed would emerge as a critical issue in the case.

The inquiry concluded on Saturday afternoon, December 4, 1948, with a finding that sufficient evidence existed to commit Alfred Beaton to trial in the Supreme Court of Newfoundland on the charge that "the said accused at Norris Arm, on the 23rd day of October, 1948, did murder one Dorothea Manuel against the Peace of our Lord the King, His Crown and Dignity."

Abbott concluded the inquiry at 4 p.m. Gillingham and Warford took custody of the prisoner and escorted him on the 5 p.m. train to His Majesty's Penitentiary in St. John's.

People in Norris Arm and elsewhere turned their attention temporarily to the coming Christmas season.

In 1948 Newfoundlanders and Labradorians celebrated their last Christmas under the governor and Commission of Government system, which had managed the colony since 1934. The debate over the colony's future political status had raged in communities large and small on the island and in Labrador since 1946. In some places, like Twillingate, the debate gave way to violence when supporters of confederation with Canada disrupted meetings of those advocating a return to responsible government.

The referendum of June 3, 1948, asked people to decide on one of three options: responsible government as it existed before 1933, confederation with Canada, or continuation of Commission of Government. An unprecedented 88.35 per cent of eligible voters showed up to cast ballots. The result showed no clear majority; but with "continuation of Commission" as the least popular option, it was dropped from the ballot and a second referendum declared for July 22.

Again the turnout was huge, at 84.39 per cent of eligible voters. Confederation carried the day by a majority of 52.34 per cent in the final tally. Negotiations began for Newfoundland's entry into the Canadian fold. Just before the Christmas season, the Newfoundland delegation, which included Joseph Smallwood, Gordon Bradley, and Albert Walsh, returned from Ottawa with the Terms of Union with Canada. If all went according to plan, Newfoundland would enter confederation as the 10th province on April 1, 1949.

Seven

Capital punishment is the most premeditated
of murders.

—Albert Camus

As 1949 arrived, the Supreme Court of Newfoundland began to prepare for what was thought to be a routine case of murder in a far-off corner of the colony. Witness statements from the preliminary inquiry in Grand Falls in early December appeared to point clearly to the guilt of the accused. The trial was set to begin at 10 a.m. on January 31.

Emerson, who had led the prosecution of Herbert Spratt in 1942, now sat as chief justice of the Supreme Court. His immediate concern was the appointment of legal counsel for the accused, whose family did not have a clear knowledge of the legal system nor the financial means to hire a defence lawyer for the trial.

The court, with the approval of the Commission of Government, settled on the team of Isaac Mercer, Arthur Mifflin, and Fabian O'Dea from the law firm of Mercer, Mifflin, and O'Dea. Newspaper accounts noted that O'Dea had just been admitted to the bar and this would be his first case. The law firm's stellar reputation, however, had already been established. Mifflin's first priority after interviewing Alfred Beaton at the penitentiary was to travel to Norris Arm to interview witnesses and to gain a clear understanding of the environment and the circumstances under which the murder had taken place.

Sir Albert Walsh, who had taken over as Commissioner of Justice and attorney general in 1947, would head the prosecution team at the trial. Walsh had begun his career as a teacher and principal in Harbour Grace but in 1924 entered law school at Dalhousie University. He became a successful lawyer and, predictably, an elected politician, serving in the stormy final term of the Richard Squires administration from 1928 to 1932. Walsh lost his seat in the election of 1932 but went on to serve as a magistrate for seven years in Grand Falls and Corner Brook. In 1940 he returned to St. John's as a senior official in the office of the Commissioner of Justice and Defence.

H.P. Carter, who had assisted in the prosecution of Herbert Spratt in 1942, was still Director of Public Prosecutions in 1948. He had steered proceedings at the magisterial inquiry in Grand Falls and would assist Walsh at the Beaton trial.

Monday, January 31, marked a week of unsettled weather across the island. Temperatures dipped to -20 degrees Fahrenheit in Norris Arm and Botwood, but forecasts on the Avalon called for milder weather with strong winds and a mixture of snow and sleet. Despite less-than-ideal conditions, a large crowd filled the lobby of the Supreme Court Building, while others gathered outside. When the courtroom doors opened, the gallery immediately filled to overflowing.

Interest in the murder trial had reached a fever pitch in and around the city. People were tired of the endless bitter debate over union with Canada which had dominated the airwaves and newspapers for two years. The story of murder in far-off Norris Arm had all the elements of a serial thriller: a young man crazed by jealousy stabs his girlfriend, a shooting rampage through town ends in the murder of a young mother, and the heroic action of a Newfoundland Ranger prevents further tragedy.

Chief Justice Emerson signalled the beginning of proceedings at 10 a.m. The clerk of the court read the formal indictment charging Alfred Beaton with the wilful murder of Dorothea Manuel on October 23, 1948, at Norris Arm. Mifflin rose on behalf of his client with a plea of not guilty.

The first 90 minutes were largely taken up with the selection of a jury from a pool of 82 men (women could not serve on juries in Newfoundland until 1972). The 12 jurors, all from St. John's, were George Marshall, Michael Skiffington, Stephen French, Ian Dunn, George Brown, Fred Udle, Harry Wareham, Alfred Streeter, Chesley Benson, John Marshall, Donald Badcock, and Edward Ash.

Carter opened the case for the crown, describing Beaton's actions from the time he left Ryan's beer parlour to his arrest by Gillingham at the east end of Range Road. The prosecutor highlighted the murder of

Dorothea Manuel, "who was walking with her husband near her home when she was shot down." He then painted a vivid picture of Gillingham's brush with death during the arrest when "Beaton fired a shot at him at close range, the bullet passing between the Ranger's side and his arm."

Carter called Capt. Glendenning as his first witness. Glendenning introduced a map of Norris Arm as well as photographs of critical areas of the community which would help the court understand the sequence of events. These included pictures of the Range, the homes that had been struck by gunfire, and the scene of the arrest.

The morning session of the court concluded at 1 p.m., and when it reconvened at 2:30 p.m. Glendenning continued his testimony. He described the weapon used during the crime, "a 44.40 Winchester lever action carbine. The rifle will hold ten shells, this type of rifle is regarded in the heavy class and is used for big game and seal hunting in this country … effective up to 500 yards."

Gillingham appeared next for the prosecution and added more detail to the diagrams of Norris Arm introduced earlier by Glendenning. Gillingham described his race, along with William Beason and John Stuckless, to stop an unknown gunman who was stalking the community.

Late on day one of the trial Sir Albert Walsh, lead prosecutor, began the questioning of other crown witnesses. Irven Manuel, first cousin of the accused, took the stand. He testified that early in the afternoon of October 23, Alfred Beaton had come to his house to help him with construction of a barn. Before beginning the work on the barn sometime between 2 and 3 p.m., Manuel now testified that they had both consumed three glasses of homebrew—a contradiction of earlier testimony given at the preliminary inquiry. Around 5 p.m., they stopped work and had another three glasses of homebrew, at which point Beaton went home for the evening meal. Manuel added that Beaton returned around 7 p.m., had another glass of homebrew, and they listened to the Doyle News Bulletin on the radio.

Manuel testified that he did not notice any change in Beaton's behaviour as a result of the drinking. They left together to visit Art Robinson's, where they had more to drink. Manuel earlier told the court that Beaton had had just one glass of homebrew at the Robinson home— again a departure from his testimony at the Grand Falls inquiry. Under cross-examination by Mifflin he admitted to seeing Beaton have "two glasses, maybe more."

Day one of the trial concluded with Manuel's describing the events at Ryan's parlour after he and Beaton had arrived there sometime after 9 p.m.

By the second day of the trial, interest in the case was building. Both of the major papers in St. John's devoted front-page coverage to the proceedings and the evening radio news programs on VOCM and on the BCN network delivered up-to-the-minute accounts to people across the island and in Labrador. In its February 2 edition, the *Evening Telegram* described the developing public fascination with the story:

> Regardless of the adverse weather conditions, the Supreme courtroom was jammed with spectators who came from near and far to hear the trial of Alfred Beaton of Norris Arm on a charge of murder. Two of the spectators came all the way from Kelligrews especially to hear the proceedings of the trial.

Mifflin's cross-examination of Irven Manuel continued on the second day of the trial with further questions about Beaton's behaviour on the night of the murder. Manuel revealed that, after the stabbing, he was making his way to Stan Goodyear's to see his girlfriend when he met Beaton again:

> I met him east of Basha's Garage. He ran down across the road a hundred feet or more. I was seven or eight feet from him. He spoke to me there, he asked me where I was going. I told him it was none of his business.... His voice sounded different. If I hadn't seen him I would not have been able to tell who it was. I was scared by the strange sound of his voice. It was an angry voice, not like the voice of Alf Beaton.

These chilling details were significantly at odds with the testimony Manuel had given during his examination at the preliminary inquiry in December. At that time, he'd said, "There was no difference in Alf Beaton's tone of voice at this time than when he had been speaking to me before, during the day."

Carter called Margaret Stuckless to the stand midway through the morning of February 1. As the first victim of Beaton's violence and his steady girlfriend for 18 months, her story was eagerly anticipated. She testified that Beaton did not seem angry or speak roughly to her when he asked who she wanted, "Jim or [him]."

"I thought he was fooling," she told the court. She then gave a detailed account of the next few violent seconds. As she turned to go home, Beaton grabbed her arm, turned her around and something smashed into her face. The spectators hung on every word as Margaret described the force of the blow as the knife blade hit her cheekbone and broke from the handle. Near tears, she described the feeling of the blade sticking in her face just below the left eye. It was only when she raised her hand to her face, she told the court, that she realized she had been stabbed.

Under cross-examination, Mercer asked Margaret whether she could think of any reason for the attack. She attempted an answer but quickly put her hands to her face and broke into tears. The chief justice ordered a 10-minute recess. When court resumed, Margaret told Mercer that she did not understand why Beaton had attacked her.

Jim Dwyer, who took the stand at 1 p.m. when court resumed for the afternoon session, testified that on October 23 he was ill, and after walking some 40 miles from his job in Gander two days earlier, he was still quite tired. He told the court that normally he would not have been at Ryan's parlour that night but because of the railway strike he had no way of getting back to his job.

Dwyer described the scene outside the beer parlour when he left to go home. He had just gone down the steps, he said, when he saw the accused and Margaret Stuckless standing about 30 feet away. Beaton said, "Come here, Jim." He walked toward them and was no more than 6 or 7 feet away when Margaret screamed. Within seconds he was dazed by a powerful blow to the side of his head. When he recovered his senses, Beaton was nowhere in sight.

Dwyer told the court that as he made his way back to his home, he heard steps behind him and a voice saying, "I'll get you." Under cross-examination by Mercer, Dwyer could not say definitely that it was Alfred

Beaton's voice.

One of the youngest witnesses for the crown took the stand after Jim Dwyer. Marie Beaton, the 15-year-old sister of the accused, testified that her father, Frank, was away working in Glenwood on October 23. Her mother had died two years earlier. Her sister, Margaret, 23 years old, and young brother, Francis, just eight, were sitting down to supper when Alfred came home around 6 p.m. after being gone all afternoon.

Marie claimed that she knew that Alfred had been drinking when he came home. She told the court that her brother left immediately after supper and returned again at 9:30 p.m. He went directly to his bedroom without speaking to her, grabbed her father's 44.40 rifle, and started loading it with shells as he came out.

Marie remained composed on the stand as defence attorney O'Dea questioned her on the number of shells Alfred had loaded into the magazine of the rifle. She could only respond that it was more than one. Later, she heard shots which seemed to come from down near the railway station but she could not recall how many shots.

O'Dea also zeroed in on Alfred's manner as he left the house. Marie said that her brother would not answer her when she asked him where he was going. "He appeared angry. I did not see him like this before."

The crown called 15-year-old Leonard Beaton as the final witness for the day. Questioned by Carter, he described to a hushed courtroom his two encounters with his cousin that night. After the first encounter, Leonard told the court he thought Alfred was out with the gun looking for his father. After he heard shots farther up the road, he and his mother decided they would be safer if they tried to get to the Goodyear home up by the hangar. They took a punt and rowed up rather than risk walking along the main road.

Carter pressed the young witness on whether he noticed anything unusual in Alfred's tone of voice. Leonard did not answer the prosecutor's question. The stress had become overwhelming. He lowered his head and cried. Court adjourned until 10 a.m., Wednesday, February 3.

By Wednesday, February 3, the trial had riveted the attention of the entire city. When Leonard Beaton resumed his testimony at 10 a.m., the gallery and the main body of the courtroom were blocked with spectators. Many others in the lobby and outside on the street could not be admitted. For the first time in several years, politics occupied second place in the public mind.

Leonard told the court of his frightening encounter with a gunman. At this point, he recounted, he did not know the identity of the person who had fired on him at point-blank range as he was trying to get to the Flynn house to warn his father. The man said, "OK, son." He described seeing the flame from the barrel of the rifle no more than a few feet in front of him. The shock wave pulled him sideways as the bullet tore through his clothing. He turned and ran back to the Goodyear house. The next morning, he discovered the bullet holes in his clothing.

Under cross-examination by O'Dea, Leonard confirmed what some other witnesses had noticed about Beaton:

> When he was speaking to me his voice was rough and kind of mad. I went into my house and told my mother I was going for the Ranger as I was afraid he was after father. When I came out I heard a voice up by Jim Dwyer's on the height. I heard someone talking a lot. I thought it was two persons. It seemed that one was answering back another. It was Alfred Beaton. I thought the Ranger was talking to him. The voice was like a person crazy.

Sam Elliot, who followed Leonard Beaton on the stand, told a similar story of his encounter with Beaton. On the night of October 23, he told the court, he had been at home listening to the radio when he heard the first gunshots at around 9:45 p.m. "I had never heard shots around Norris Arm at night before," said Elliot. "I figured there was something strange going on." He rushed outside and walked about 10 feet up the road when he saw a man in front of him. The man said, "stick 'em up," and several more shots were fired. He identified the voice as that of Alfred Beaton. Elliot said he ran back inside the house, put out the lights, and told his wife and children to get away from the windows. In response to a question from Mercer on how Beaton sounded, Elliot said:

> The voice seemed angry and rough … I have known Alfred Beaton since he was a small boy, he is ordinarily a bit low speaking. His voice was louder, voice sounded

very rough, savage to me. I could not say Alfred Beaton was drunk. It sounded crazy. It appeared to me that he meant business. I have no explanation …

Johanna Manuel, mother of Irven Manuel, followed Elliot on the witness stand. She testified that when Beaton came back to her house around 7 p.m. he had had more than one glass of beer but she did not know how many. He left with her son about 8:15 p.m. but did not seem intoxicated.

Johanna told the court she had been sewing at home later that night when she was startled by gunshots. She went outside to see what was going on and saw a figure running down the road. She did not recognize him at first but as he came nearer she saw that it was her nephew, Alfred Beaton.

She remembered saying, "Alfred, give me the gun. I'll take it in the house and you can get it in the morning."

She told the court that Beaton ignored her and she said again, "Alfred, give me the gun."

Johanna stated that Beaton refused her pleas and instead pointed to the sky and said, "Don't you see all that up there? I've got to have all that tonight before I'm finished." As he walked away, she said, he looked back at her and shouted, "Don't shed any tears for me tonight."

Johanna said she felt extremely upset by the encounter and feared what might happen next. Later that night she learned that Dorothea Manuel had been killed.

In response to a question from O'Dea, Johanna said she did not understand what Beaton was talking about when he pointed to the sky. She thought he was crazy.

Ruby Elliot testified after Johanna Manuel. She told the court she had been at Ryan's parlour that night with Margaret Stuckless and had rushed outside when she heard her friend's screams. She took Margaret to Mrs. Budgell's for treatment and stayed there to offer assistance. Hallett and Dorothea Manuel arrived much later and, when they left to go home, she and Annie Stuckless had left with them. Ruby noted that everyone was very upset and uneasy about the gunfire in the community.

She testified that they had gone only a short distance when a shot rang out close by. She described her panic after the blast as she and Annie ran for the shelter of the nearest house. When she looked back, she saw Dorothea on the ground with her husband kneeling over her. Ruby said she clearly remembered turning around and going back to Budgell's and being in the house just as Allan and Gilbert Purchase brought in Dorothea's body.

Annie Stuckless, Margaret's mother, was the fifth witness at the morning session. Her brief testimony confirmed that of Ruby Elliot. She said that she had walked to Mrs. Budgell's that night to see her daughter after learning about the stabbing and was relieved that Margaret was not in a lot of pain. They left the house thinking there was safety in numbers, never realizing the danger. No one had a flashlight because the night was not real dark. She told the court she was walking to the left of Dorothea Manuel, "with her right shoulder touching my left shoulder ... When the shot was fired Mrs. Manuel fell to the ground, I looked at her while she was on the ground and there was blood coming from her mouth."

The highly anticipated testimony of Hallett Manuel, the victim's husband, began shortly before noon. The court heard that not only had he lost his wife but their two young sons aged seven and two had lost their mother. He described the moments after the fatal shot when he realized that his wife was critically injured: "I laid her on the ground and kept her head up, I then felt the back part of her coat getting wet ... the part around her shoulders. I then realized she had been hit."

Manuel continued his testimony when court reconvened for the afternoon session. He told the court that with the assistance of two other men he carried his wife into Mrs. Budgell's home, where she died shortly after. There was no cross-examination.

Stan Langdon took the stand next. He testified that he had heard seven or eight shots that night. The first two, he said, came from the far eastern end of Norris Arm and to him sounded muffled, like someone dropping lumber. Just along Range Road from his house he joined a group of men talking about the gunfire but became nervous and went back home. He told the court that the location of his home at the far end of Range Road made him a witness to the tragic end of the drama and the arrest of the gunman:

> I heard another shot. It seemed to come right by the east
> corner of my house ... afterwards I heard another shot

which appeared to come from the east but it was muffled. I was in the house then when I heard some person say, "Halt," and then I went out the back door and I heard someone say, "Hold him, John." I recognized the voice as that of Ranger Gillingham.

Langdon said that he then went back inside and told his wife that the gunman had been caught. He went out his front door to see what the commotion was just down Range Road: "Some person flashed a light ... and I recognized one of the two people on the road as Hallett Manuel, and he was laid across the other person. I then heard him tell the person with the flashlight that she was shot."

John Stuckless took the stand as the final witness for the prosecution on day three of the trial. He told the court that he had participated in the tragic events from the time that his sister was stabbed outside Ryan's parlour until the capture and transportation of the prisoner to the jail in Botwood. After realizing that a gunman was on the loose, Gillingham asked him and William Beason for their help in tracking down whoever it was.

Stuckless outlined his role in assisting with the arrest of Beaton: "I heard the Ranger say, 'I got him, John,' and we ran up to where the Ranger was. We held Beaton, the Ranger handcuffed him and we took him to the station." Under cross-examination, Stuckless told the court that Beaton appeared very angry when he was arrested. As they were escorting him down to the government wharf for the boat trip to Botwood, Beaton kept mumbling but Stuckless could not understand anything he was saying.

On Thursday, February 3, the trial entered its fourth day, with no lessening of public interest. Rumours that Beaton himself would take the stand added to the attention given to the drama unfolding at the Supreme Court Building on Duckworth Street. Crowds still packed the public gallery and many more waited patiently outside.

Stuckless returned to the stand for further cross-examination. Mercer wanted more details of the moments before the arrest. Stuckless told the court that when they began to move in on the gunman Gillingham was in possession of both a rifle and a revolver. Before moving toward the sound of the shooting, Gillingham handed the rifle to him with the words, "If the man gets me, you get him." At this point, he said, they did not know the identity of the gunman.

William Beason, who appeared next, corroborated Stuckless's testimony, adding several more details of the arrest. He told the court that Beaton was angry and refused to walk after he was handcuffed. A slap from Gillingham was enough to get the accused moving.

At mid-morning Ranger Bruce Gillingham took the stand to describe in more detail the race to stop a gunman in Norris Arm on the night of October 23, 1948. When he had first learned of the stabbing, he went directly to Mrs. Budgell's home to see the victim, Margaret Stuckless. He left Budgell's intending to arrest Beaton at his home, but when he reached the main road, William Beason met him and told him there was shooting down east.

Gillingham told the court he decided immediately that he needed to be armed. He proceeded to Edgar Perry's house to borrow a rifle, a 44.40 Winchester, and then hurried back to his boarding house to get his own .38 revolver.

They finally narrowed the area of the gunfire to the section of the community known as the Range. It was here at the end of the main road running through the Range that Gillingham laid out a strategy to capture the gunman. Beason and Stuckless would hide behind a large boulder with the rifle at the ready and he would move cautiously forward.

Gillingham said he had gone just to the corner of a fence near Stan Langdon's house when he spotted the gunman approaching no more than 100 feet away to the west on Range Road. The man turned around and fired, then immediately turned again and ran in his direction. "I hid behind a corner of the fence," said Gillingham, "and took out my revolver."

When the man knelt to take another shot only a few feet from the corner of the fence, Gillingham decided to make his move. He described tucking his revolver back in his belt and rushing the gunman. Unfortunately, in doing so he kicked a tin can. The gunman turned with the rifle at shoulder level and fired at point-blank range. Gillingham told the court that at the time he believed he'd been hit, but later learned this was not the case.

Gillingham's story was critical to the prosecution's case. For nearly two hours Carter led him through the intense effort to locate the gunman, the arrest, the boat trip to Botwood where the accused was jailed, and the discovery on their return trip that Dorothea Manuel had been fatally shot.

When court reconvened in the afternoon, Gillingham continued his testimony. He told the court that he and Sergeant Gosling began the search for evidence early the next morning. In front of Ryan's parlour, he said, they found the blood-covered blade of the knife used in the stabbing. They found a bullet hole in a picket at the corner of the fence from which he had rushed Beaton. The knife and part of the picket were shown to the jury.

Gillingham then described their investigation at Jim Dwyer's home. The two officers noted the locations where four bullets had struck the house. A fifth was discovered later. Their evidence gathering continued until Capt. Glendenning arrived later in the afternoon to head up the investigation.

After Walsh concluded his questioning, Defence Attorney Mercer conducted an intense cross-examination of Gillingham, who had testified early in the trial that the rifle was a lever-action Winchester. In response to a question from the defence lawyer as to whether he had seen the accused use the underarm lever between the final two shots, Gillingham said that he had not. Mercer wondered whether this might indicate that another gunman was on the loose that night.

Mercer also highlighted the injuries to Beaton's face which were later treated in Grand Falls. "Had the injuries happened during or after the arrest?" asked Mercer. Gillingham replied that when he charged into Beaton, the suspect struggled to get away and he was forced to subdue him with a left-handed blow to the head, which likely caused the injury.

Dr. Gerald Smith followed Gillingham on the witness stand. Smith told the court that in the early morning hours of October 24 he was asked to go to Norris Arm. He left Botwood by boat about 1 a.m. On arrival in Norris Arm he went directly to the home of Mrs. Budgell, where he treated Margaret Stuckless for a stab wound which he did not consider life-threatening.

Smith went into another room, where he saw the body of Dorothea Manuel. "The clothes of the victim both front and back were considerably blood stained," said Smith. "I concluded that the bullet had passed from back to front." Smith reported that he believed that death was instantaneous due to internal bleeding and shock—a conclusion later confirmed by an autopsy.

Carter next called Constable Edward Bennett to the stand. Bennett reported that he searched Beaton when he was brought to the Botwood jail that night. He found in the prisoner's possession three 30.30 cartridges, some snare wire, a knife handle, a sheath for a knife, and various small items.

Bennett described Beaton's behaviour after he was taken to his cell. "He did not go to sleep but just sat on his bunk and when I did my check on the prisoner at 4:14 a.m. Beaton was still sitting on his bunk and said to me, 'It's an awful thing I've done tonight.'" Bennett maintained that he immediately asked the prisoner if he wanted to make a statement and cautioned him that anything he might say could be used in a court of law. He then took Beaton to the office, formally charged him, and repeated the caution. At that point the accused told his story non-stop, without prompting, and signed the statement after it was read back to him. Bennett read Beaton's statement to the court.

O'Dea cross-examined Bennett and questioned his version of events. The defence lawyer asserted that his client had not been cautioned, had not been read the statement before he signed it, and in fact had not understood what he was signing.

Michael Hogan, the station manager for the Newfoundland Railway at Norris Arm and the 17th and final witness for the crown, took the witness stand late in the afternoon. Hogan told the court that on October 23 Gillingham had come to the station between 11 and 11:15 p.m. with two rifles, asking him to put the weapons under lock and key until he returned from Botwood.

Hogan said that he locked the guns in the station office. Later in the night James Basha came by and, out of curiosity, wanted to see what kind of rifle had been used in the shooting. Hogan opened the office door and showed Basha the two rifles but maintained that neither of them touched the weapons. He indicated that Gillingham came back a few hours later and retrieved the guns.

When queried by O'Dea, Hogan told the court that he could clearly hear Beaton outside the station when Gillingham entered. He stated that the voice was louder than usual but not overly loud. He claimed to know Beaton well and found him to be "a very nice boy."

Walsh announced to the court that he would call no further witnesses for the crown. The dramatic climax to the trial would come the next day.

When Friday, February 4, dawned, people had already started gathering outside the entrance to the Supreme Court Building in downtown St. John's. The *Evening Telegram* reported that when the court reconvened at 10 a.m., "The gallery of the courtroom was filled and during the proceedings even the special seats before the bench were taken by visiting lawyers and other spectators." A *Daily News* reporter noted that some in the audience were women. On this day, as on the previous four, hundreds more milled about in the lobby and in the street outside, unable to gain entrance.

A buzz of anticipation filled the courtroom as Beaton took the stand in his own defence at 10 a.m. He identified himself as a lumberman from Norris Arm with two sisters and a younger brother. In terms of his actions in the community on the night of October 23, 1948, he offered few details:

> I walked over to Jim Dwyer's and Margaret Stuckless' table. I asked her to come outside, I wanted to see her. We went out and I asked her what was wrong. I don't know what she said. She left the steps to go down towards the road to go home. I remember going down so far with her. That's all I remember about that ... I remember next asking the Ranger what he had me arrested for—somewhere between Saunders & Howell's Store and the railway station. He told me he had arrested me for stabbing Margaret Stuckless.

Beaton told the court he had had at least seven glasses of beer at Irven Manuel's house where he had gone to help out with a barn. He had more—at least three—at Robinson's before going to Ryan's parlour.

After Mercer elicited these details, Walsh took the floor to ask Beaton a pointed question. Did the accused have any memory of obtaining a rifle and using it that night? Beaton maintained that he had no memory of returning to his home to obtain a gun but he did remember firing some shots into the air.

When Walsh showed the accused the signed statement he had made to Constable Bennett in the early morning of October 24, Beaton told the court he could neither read nor write but he could write his own name. He recognized his signature on the paper but claimed some of it was false and Bennett had not cautioned him at all that night.

The last witness during the trial and the only witness for the defence took the stand at 11 a.m. Margaret Beaton testified that she was Alfred's older sister and was in charge of the household in Norris Arm while her father was away at work. She expanded on the earlier testimony of her young sister, Marie, who had been on the stand earlier in the week. Margaret claimed that when her brother came home for the evening meal at 6:30 p.m. on October 23, his face was flushed and his eyes and behaviour indicated that he was intoxicated. She could plainly smell alcohol on him. He was quiet around the house and left right after supper without saying where he was going. When Margaret's brief testimony concluded at 11:10, court recessed for 20 minutes.

Isaac Mercer, senior partner on the defence team, began his address to the jury at 11:35 a.m. The burden of proof lies with the crown, he said, and the crown had produced insufficient evidence of his client's intent to murder; he barely knew the victim. There was no malice and there was no motive. Mercer asked the jury to consider several key questions:

> Did this boy deliberately set out to commit a felony in the course of which Dorothea Manuel was killed? Did the bullet from his gun kill Dorothea Manuel—there was conflicting evidence of the number of shots—by one count there were nine, other witnesses claim eleven. Where did the other two shots come from? Was the weapon taken from Beaton the same one introduced into evidence—the Ranger testified that he did not hear or see the lever action being used by his client just before the arrest.

In acknowledging that his client fired his rifle randomly on the night in question, Mercer stressed that these were the actions of a boy influenced by drunkenness and insanity. Questions remained about the amount of beer consumed by his client. By one count at least eight glasses, by another at least 12.

Mercer reminded the jury there was ample evidence of insanity—whether temporary or otherwise. Many witnesses, such as Irven Manuel, testified to the strange sound of Albert's voice; others, like Leonard Beaton, that he was talking to himself; still others like Johanna Manuel, that he made strange statements. Gillingham had testified that Alfred was in a rage when he was arrested.

The key element of intent, argued Mercer, was taken away by drunkenness and insanity.

In his closing argument, Mercer asked the jury to consider carefully whether the crown had proven beyond a reasonable doubt that the fatal shot which killed the victim came from Beaton's gun, whether there was premeditated intent, and whether the young man set out with the intention to commit a murder.

At 2:30 p.m., Sir Albert Walsh began his address to the jury on behalf of the crown. He outlined again for the court the details of Beaton's rampage through a peaceful community with a high-powered weapon, which he must have known would kill or seriously maim any person in the line of fire. The actions of the accused that night, argued Walsh, had spread fear through an entire community and resulted in the tragic death of a young wife and mother of two small children. It was only by pure chance that many others were not killed or seriously injured.

Walsh disputed the defence claim that the accused was intoxicated. Seventeen crown witnesses had testified that there was little evidence that Beaton was drunk and still less evidence that he did not know what he was doing, or that it was wrong. "The conclusion we must all make," said the prosecutor, "is that this man set out on a mission of revenge and in the process committed murder."

In his charge to the jury, Chief Justice Emerson reminded them of their heavy responsibility in deciding the fate of the accused. He outlined the difference between murder and manslaughter. If the jury was satisfied that the accused set out with the intention of committing the crime, they would have to return a verdict of guilty. If, on the other hand, they were satisfied that this was not the case, they could return a verdict of manslaughter.

Emerson reminded the jury that the defence had put forward "a plea of insanity, brought about by intoxication." "There is a further possible defence," he instructed, "that of drunkenness, which differs somewhat from insanity and does not call for such a degree of instability." If the jury accepted this defence, he explained, they would have to be satisfied that, at the time of the offence, the mind of the accused was so affected by alcohol that he was incapable of forming the intent to kill.

The jury retired at 3:50 p.m. Many of the spectators anticipated that the deliberations would be lengthy with likely no decision until the following week. Some of these left the courtroom. Most, however, stayed where they were and vacant seats were soon filled from the overflow outside.

The audience was shocked into silence when the court was suddenly called to order at 4:30 p.m. Emerson took his chair and the jury filed back into the chamber. The chair of the jury, G.W. Brown, stood and asked Emerson to explain again the nature of the law with respect to insanity. Emerson explained the M'Naghten Rules:

> In order to succeed in a plea of insanity, the accused must prove clearly to the jury that at the time when he committed the acts complained of, he was labouring under such a defect of reason from disease of the mind as not to know the nature and quality of the act he was doing, or if he did know it, that he did not know that what he was doing was wrong. The law recognizes temporary insanity and it recognizes insanity brought on by intoxication.

The jury filed out of the courtroom again. Most of the spectators were now confident that the jury had signalled their decision. They did not have long to wait.

At 5:20 p.m. word came that the jury had reached a verdict. Two police officers escorted Beaton to the prisoner's box. The 12-man jury filed back into the courtroom. When His Lordship entered the room, as one reporter said, "A hush fell over the crowd of spectators." Emerson asked the jury if they had reached a verdict.

The chair of the jury stood and replied, "We have, your honour, we find the accused guilty of murder as charged." As the chair sat down without a recommendation for mercy, there were gasps of shock from the gallery. Everyone instantly realized that the verdict meant death. Emerson first called for silence, then asked the prisoner to stand. "Alfred Beaton, you have been found guilty of the crime of murder by a jury of your countrymen. Do you have anything to say before sentence is passed?" Beaton shook his head slightly.

Emerson pronounced sentence immediately:

> This court doth ordain you, Alfred Beaton, to be taken from hence to the place from whence you came, and from there to the place of execution, and that you be there hanged by the neck until you are pronounced dead and that your body afterwards be buried within the precincts of the prison in which you shall have been confined after your conviction, and may the Lord have mercy on your soul.

The prisoner's face flushed and he clenched his hands at his side as the sentence was declared.

As Beaton walked out of the courtroom into the lobby of the Supreme Court Building, he lost his composure, sobbed uncontrollably, and covered his face with a handkerchief—a photograph of the event appeared in city newspapers the next day. His young sister, Marie, also in tears, rushed from the crowd and clung to her brother. Supported by his two police guards, Beaton was taken to the prison van waiting at the Duckworth Street entrance of the courthouse.

Weekend editions of the two major dailies in St. John's carried banner headlines of the verdict. "Alfred Beaton Convicted of Murder: Chief Justice Imposes the Death Sentence," trumpeted the *Daily News* on February 5. A picture of the distraught prisoner between two solemn police officers appeared underneath with a caption noting that "several women who were amongst the audience became very upset."

On Friday night, radio stations carried the sombre news of the death sentence across the island and into Labrador. For many in Norris Arm and in other communities in central Newfoundland, it was a shocking conclusion to the trial. Storm clouds of public discontent quickly began to gather.

On Monday, February 7, just two days after Emerson handed down the death sentence, the *Evening Telegram* printed an emotional plea for mercy in its Letters to the Editor section. The letter, written under the pen name "Portia," a Shakespearean character from *The Merchant of Venice*, became an eloquent and inspirational call to action against capital punishment in Newfoundland.

> Dear Sir,
> The decision in the recent murder trial has so affected me that I feel driven to make some comments on the principles involved, not so much that I expect these comments to have the effect of diverting the course of justice, but mainly I suppose I feel in duty bound to give voice to the emotions which arise in me while I admit to the sincere hope that my effort will have the effect of snowballing on the tide of public opinion and sympathy to the desired goal of attaining for an unfortunate fellow being, a measure of mercy, so desirable and so sweet.
>
> In the first place let me say that it is the principle involved and not the method which, to my mind, is in error. By this I mean that to my way of thinking the members of the jury and the Chief Justice are absolved from any measure of responsibility in the matter insofar as they were, each in their appointed spheres, honestly following the dictates of a clearly defined legal procedure which states that the British courts must exact an eye for an eye and a tooth for a tooth.
>
> Now, while I have the deepest and most profound respect for practically every form of British law, I sincerely feel that that statute which imposes the penalty of death on a human being was compounded at a time when the meagre value placed on human life and the laxity of legal protection were such as to make brutality

a necessary part of law enforcement.

I must proclaim, with all the powers which my sadly inadequate pen can command, that in these supposedly enlightened and more civilized times we can surely afford to temper our justice with mercy.

The fact that the world is beginning to react to the repugnance of a statute which calls for a human sacrifice is apparent in that strong forces are now at work within the framework of the British Parliament to abolish the death sentence, and I maintain that in our little country where crimes of violence are so singularly rare as to be almost non-existent, it is nothing short of barbarism for our courts to cling to a statute which was conceived in desperation in an age of violence.

Surely in a Christian country such as ours, we cannot with impunity and sincerity venture to claim for the state that vengeance which is God's alone. I cannot conceive that any worldly agency can, or should attempt to embrace the awful power to project a mortal being into the abyss of eternity for an offence against the laws of man, and if this punishment is being enforced for an offence against the laws of God, then the punishment should surely be left in His hands.

I am not trying to weigh the merits of the case of the crown vs. Alfred Beaton, and if I were to apply an impartial, worldly analysis to the case I would probably come to the same reluctant conclusion, in the face of the facts presented, as that arrived at by the members of the jury. What I am trying to do is to outline as vividly as possible, against a background of social justice in a community where Christian principles are still, supposedly, the guiding ones, the narrow and illegible line which divides medieval brutality from true justice.

I am personally convinced that Alfred Beaton wilfully and callously took the life of a human being in what would appear to be a fit of uncontrollable temper, and further, that in so doing he brought irremediable suffering and heartache to others—inoffensive victims, innocent of fault—and for this Alfred Beaton must accept the severest of punishments, not for any mistaken concept of vengeance, but because in all justice the punishment must, insofar as possible fit the crime.

I clearly realize that extraordinary measures are necessary and indeed vital in dealing with humans who cross the border of rational behaviour to such an extent as to take a life. Obviously society must be protected against such extremes and the only solution which can appease the hunger of the world for justice without offering offense to God is to deprive the criminal for the rest of his life of social privileges by confining him to prison for life.

This is a punishment understandable and even acceptable to the human mind with all its frailties and the criminal who takes a life has no right to expect less.

Perhaps the saddest and most regrettable fact of the present case is the fact that the defendant is so obviously helpless to present a clear picture of the forces which drive him to commit this great offense because of his youth and his regrettable illiteracy.

Is it not a reflection on the rest of us that we can see fit to leave one of our own charges to flounder as best he can along the hard road of life without enlightenment or assistance, only to pounce upon him with righteous indignation when his neglected steps lead him across the line of convention which we have laid down?

This is probably the only country in the world where practically every citizen professes to believe in the immortality of the soul and the existence of a God Who is as all merciful as He is all just. Should not the laws of the land then be so devised, without impairing their efficiency, as to be harmonious with the spiritual beliefs of the people for whom they are instituted?

I have never made a study of the law (a fact which is probably obvious to those who have) and already I feel sure that many who read this letter will say that I am over-presumptive in assuming that I am competent to suggest that there is something in our legal code which is hideous and unjust, but I would ask them to remember that I am considering the interpretation in the light in which it applies to our people in Newfoundland not as it applies in countries where, among teeming millions, there exist many dangerous elements which respect no law but the law of brute force.

My own conviction is that capital punishment is wrong anywhere, but in a predominantly Christian land such as ours it is in direct juxtaposition to the moral and spiritual principles of the people.

Let our laws be just and inexorable, but let their jurisdiction be limited to the confines of this world. It is my sincere belief that I am reflecting the sentiments of the majority of our people.

For the obvious reason that my sincerity may be misconstrued as a particularly callous attempt to achieve the limelight I am remaining anonymous. To those of you who have read this letter and who feel as I do, I appeal to you to express these sentiments in the press.

It is my belief that the impending tragic event may still be circumvented. If you believe as I do that this punishment is excessive then it is your solemn duty—note well the words—your solemn duty, to register your protest.

Remember, a life may be in the balance and you have no moral right to ignore the possibility. No matter how inarticulate you may be, it is the main thought, your repugnance against capital punishment, which is important; the amount of public support which is vital.

If my inadequate plea has been in vain, then I say now to Alfred Beaton that I hope and pray that you are a believer in God for in His mercy alone can you find comfort; certainly there can be none in the sterile realization that you are the victim of a system which desires to give to Caesar that which is God's.

PORTIA

Portia's letter was the first move in the battle to save Alfred Beaton from the hangman.

Events moved swiftly behind the scenes in the office of Governor Macdonald and the Commission of Government. Six years earlier, in the Herbert Spratt case, an indignant Chief Justice Horwood took a full seven days to deliver his report to Governor Walwyn. The trial itself, which lasted just under two days, resulted in a rush to conviction and an execution only 24 days later.

On Monday afternoon, February 7, 1949, Emerson delivered his report to Macdonald in compliance with the terms outlined in the Letters Patent issued by the British government in January 1934. The next morning, Kenneth Macdonald, the governor's private secretary, circulated the report to the six commissioners of the government.

Emerson began his report on a positive note, emphasizing that "Alfred Beaton is a young man of nineteen years of age ... a lumberman who is neither able to read nor write, except that he can write his signature ... his character appears to have been good and he is described by a witness as being decent and quiet." The report provided a detailed account of the actions of the convicted man on October 23, 1948.

Emerson disputed defence claims of intoxication as a factor in the murder. Beaton had consumed at least eight glasses of homebrew at Irven Manuel's house but, according to Manuel, the "concoction" had only been brewing for 24 hours. Emerson wondered whether this was enough time to develop much alcoholic content. "For myself, I doubt it very much," he said. Beaton consumed a further four glasses at the home of Connors and Robinson but most witnesses, with the exception of his sister, Margaret, testified that he did not appear intoxicated.

There was also scant evidence, reported Emerson, for the defence claim that their client suffered from insanity at the time of the murder—at least not enough evidence to satisfy the jury.

Emerson also expressed his annoyance at the defence lawyers in the case "for unduly prolonging the trial by the unnecessarily detailed cross-examination." The criticism was tempered with the observation that the final speech for the defence "was carefully thought out and covered every point that it was possible to urge on behalf of the accused."

Emerson concluded his trial report to Macdonald with his opinion that the verdict of the jury was justified by the evidence.

On the same day Macdonald's office received a review of the material evidence from the Commissioner of Justice Sir Albert Walsh, who had served as chief prosecutor at the trial. The review supported information already provided in the report of Emerson. Walsh emphasized that the jury, in finding Beaton guilty of murder, made no recommendation for mercy. He insisted that this was the right decision:

> There is no doubt that the verdict of the jury was the proper one in this case. The evidence established clearly that the accused killed Dorothea Manuel and that the killing was not accidental or provoked. While the accused had consumed a quantity of beer the evidence indicated that it would not have had more than a moderately intoxicating effect if taken in short periods.... There was little if any evidence on which a jury could reach the conclusion that this man was insane within the legal definition.

Immediately following sentencing, the governor's office began information gathering from a wide range of professionals outside the justice system. Early on Monday, Dr. Charles A. Roberts, superintendent of the Hospital for Mental and Nervous Diseases, delivered his assessment of the prisoner. Roberts had examined Beaton immediately before the trial and found no evidence of "psychosis or gross mental defectiveness." He did acknowledge, however, that the prisoner showed a degree of immaturity, "but not such as would make one consider him to be in any way not responsible for his actions."

Dr. E. Leo Sharpe, general medical superintendent and prison physician, delivered his report on the same day. Sharpe informed the governor that, in his opinion, Beaton was in good health and of sound mind. He conceded, however, that while he could find no mental defects, Beaton "appears to be of a rather low grade of intelligence—due, no doubt, to lack of education, combined with associating in an undesirable environment."

W.F. Case, superintendent of His Majesty's Penitentiary, delivered his report on Tuesday, February 8. Case indicated that since Beaton had arrived at the prison on December 5, 1948, he had been under constant guard and observation: "There were no symptoms of insanity ... I have had several conversations with him myself and noticed nothing abnormal about him."

Case's assessment noted that when Beaton returned to the prison immediately after the conviction he showed considerable signs of distress, "which under the circumstances would be expected. I visit him once or twice daily since then and he displays little or no emotion."

The eloquent appeal for mercy by Portia, which appeared in the *Evening Telegram* on February 7, 1949, sparked an avalanche of letters to the editor in both St. John's dailies and in regional weeklies like the *Grand Falls Advertiser* and the *Twillingate Sun*. Even letters expressing opinions on the hot-button issue of confederation were now crowded out as concerned citizens came out in support of Portia's stand.

One "Fair-minded Citizen" argued that the death sentence should be commuted to life imprisonment. "We wish to voice our repugnance at the sentence handed down in the case of the nineteen-year-old Alfred Beaton," stated the writer. "We think the sentence might have been tempered with a recommendation for mercy."

"Portia, I salute you for your courageous stand," said another writer under the pen name "Mercy." The individual asked the *Evening Telegram* to throw the full weight of the newspaper behind the campaign against capital punishment. Using a biblical reference, Mercy reminded readers that "God, the author of life, did not exact the death of Cain for his foul deed, rather He banished Cain from society."

Other writers like "VOX POPULI, VOX DEI" (The voice of the people is the voice of God) stressed that Beaton must be punished, for "justice demands punishment." However, hanging a 19-year-old was not the answer, argued the writer. "Since life is God given, only God should have the power to take it away."

In the February 10 edition of the *Evening Telegram*, an anonymous writer, P.M.M., begged for mercy for "the unfortunate nineteen-year-old boy, Alfred Beaton." The writer supported long prison sentences for murder and expressed his or her revulsion for hanging: "The thought of capital punishment fills me with horror ... even in cases of coldly premeditated murder."

"Gratiano," a character from the same Shakespearean play as Portia, took a more poetic bent in his or her letter to the editor. "Spare his poor life," begged the writer, "but let him never more know the happiness of walking at liberty through Newfoundland's green fields and leafy woods and sailing over her water." This writer complimented his or her fellow character: "If 'Portia' has never made a study of the law, Newfoundland is the poorer."

Most letters to the editor, while calling for mercy, also expressed sympathy for the victim. "Who should receive more sympathy," queried one writer, "the young man at the bar of justice or the victim whose life was taken? A young married woman living a useful life in that state of life ordained by God fell in her husband's arms without warning and without a chance of uttering the last prayer to the creator ..."

Another writer, who had closely followed the trial proceedings, stressed that Beaton was insane at the time of the murder and "crazed by drink." If the murder had been premeditated, the writer argued, nobody would stand up for him, "but if Dorothea Manuel could speak from her quiet grave do you think she would ask that the extreme penalty be exacted? I think not. I feel very strongly that she would not."

Many people were deeply moved by Portia's appeal for mercy. Most struggled to find in the tragedy some larger lessons for individual families and Newfoundland society in general. For others, Beaton rapidly became a symbol of the many things that were wrong as everyone rushed to embrace the modern world. "Could it be that the cause of all this may be the beer shops?" asked one correspondent. Another wondered whether the government itself was to blame by increasing its revenue through its dealing in "the accursed drink traffic."

Some newspapers featured articles on the root causes of juvenile delinquency, pointing the finger squarely at the breakdown of authority and discipline in the home and in the schools. Editorials condemned the violence in motion pictures, comic books, and radio programs. One editor encouraged more recreation facilities "which would channel youthful energy into healthier and more constructive pursuits."

By Saturday, February 12, major papers were beginning to respond to public pressure. The conservative *Daily News*, in its editorial, acknowledged the growing movement against capital punishment, stating that most people believed life imprisonment should be the maximum penalty. The editor, however, argued there was still a place for "the full penalty of the law" in a case of deliberately planned murder. "The situation is far different," he said, "when the murder is not premeditated."

The *Grand Falls Advertiser* on February 19 took a more vigorous stand against the extreme penalty. "The death penalty," said the editor, "was conceived as a desperate measure for a violent age—a time of violence which has little resemblance to life as it is lived today on this God fearing island ..." His thoughts echoed those of Portia.

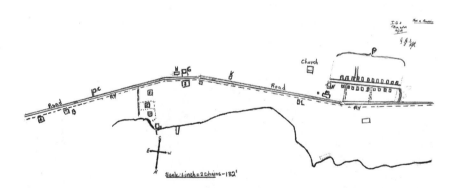

Hand-drawn map used in evidence at the Beaton trial. The main road and railway ran parallel to each other through the community. The Range appears at the right, marked P. Frank Beaton's home is at the top, marked A. Michael Ryan's parlour is left centre, marked G.

The row of company houses in Norris Arm known as the Range. *Supreme Court of Newfoundland and Labrador*

The Goodyear house near the Hanger, Norris Arm, 1948. *Supreme Court of Newfoundland and Labrador*

The crime scene: Range Road looking east; entrance to the Budgell home is between the logs and large boulder. *Supreme Court of Newfoundland and Labrador*

Alfred Beaton arrives for trial at the Supreme Court of Newfoundland. Evening Telegram, *January 31, 1949*

Witnesses from Norris Arm, left to right: Marie Beaton, Ruby Elliot, Margaret Stuckless, Annie Stuckless, and Johanna Manuel. Daily News, *February 2, 1949*

Witnesses from Norris Arm, left to right: Jim Dwyer, Irvin Manuel, Hallett Manuel, and Leonard Beaton. Daily News, *February 2, 1949*

Alfred Beaton after receiving the death sentence. Daily News, *February 5, 1949*

Sir Gordon and Lady Macdonald from a family photograph of the early 1940s. Their daughter Elsie is on the far left. Standing left to right: sons, Ramsey and Kenneth, daughter Glenys. Kenneth and Glenys accompanied their father to Newfoundland. *Photograph provided by the Hon. Susan Stride*

Commission of Government for Newfoundland, November 1946. Left to right: Hon. J.S. Neill, Commissioner of Public Utilities and Supply; Hon. A.J. Walsh, Commissioner of Home Affairs and Education; Sir John Puddester, Commissioner of Public Health and Welfare; W.J. Carew, Secretary to the Commission; Governor Sir Gordon Macdonald; Hon. H.A. Winter, Commissioner of Justice; Hon. W.H. Finn, Commissioner of Natural Resources; and Hon. R.L.M. James, Commissioner of Finance and Customs. *The Rooms Provincial Archives Division, C 5-104*

St. John's waterfront, August 1945, with the Newfoundland Supreme Court Building in the background. *The Rooms Provincial Archives Division, VA 15a-48.3*

A Newfoundland Ranger at St. Anthony, August 1937. *The Rooms Provincial Archives Division, VA 124-36.1*

Overlapping the press campaign, youth organizations in St. John's spearheaded the circulation of petitions denouncing the sentence of death passed on Alfred Beaton. During the second week of February, young people motivated by Portia's call to action canvassed businesses, public gatherings, and pedestrians on city streets, gathering signatures in support of a reprieve. By Friday, February 11, 50 petitions, each with space for 300 signatures, were circulating in St. John's. Residents of Norris Arm and other communities across Newfoundland requested that petitions be sent to them as well.

Letters to the editor cheered on the resourcefulness of young people in the city and requested all mothers and fathers, "some of you with boys of nineteen in their junior year at the university, give your signatures with a prayer for mercy when you are asked to sign the petition."

A few individuals thought that the petitioners went too far in calling for a blanket abolition of the death penalty. Despite their misgivings, however, they supported the plea of mercy toward Beaton based on "the extreme youth of the lad, his unfortunate environment, his lack of education and Christian training."

Beaton's legal team, Mercer, Mifflin, and O'Dea, announced immediately after the trial that they would file an appeal on behalf of their client. They spent the week of February 7 preparing their argument. On Saturday, February 12, they presented the appeal to the Supreme Court of Newfoundland and asked that the conviction be set aside.

The lawyers laid out arguments for the appeal: there was no evidence, they maintained, that their client had intended to kill the deceased or that he deliberately shot at four people on the road, but there was sufficient evidence that their client was suffering from a mental disease induced by liquor to such an extent that he did not know what he was doing and that it was wrong.

While these were important issues at trial, the substance of the appeal by Beaton's legal team consisted of errors they claimed were made by Emerson in his instruction to the jury: that he merely put to the jury his own view of the facts without putting forth all the evidence; that he failed to instruct the jury on the distinction between drunkenness and insanity induced by liquor; and that his instructions tended to confuse, rather than clarify, the legal issues involved.

The defence team also questioned Emerson's omissions: On the charge of murder, for example, he did not tell the jury that the burden of proof rested with the crown; and, secondly, he did not explain what was meant by "disease of the mind." The team went one step further, alleging that

> The learned trial judge misdirected the jury when he said in part, "if any person deliberately shoots a rifle at three or four persons walking along a street and kills one." In that such a remark tended to convey to the minds of the jury that there was evidence that the accused saw the people on the road and deliberately shot at them but he failed to remind the jury that there was no direct evidence of such knowledge or intention on the part of the accused.

It was the first appeal of its kind to be filed in a Newfoundland court. Despite the request that the sentence be set aside and the snowballing public outcry against capital punishment, the fate of Alfred Beaton still lay in the balance.

Given Sir Gordon Macdonald's experience as a labour leader, politician, and senior manager for the wartime government of Great Britain, he was not one to waver in his decision making, nor to hide his stand on critical concerns of the day. In 1949 St. John's, a city with a small-town mentality, everyone knew where the governor stood on important issues like Confederation, poverty, and the death penalty.

On Wednesday, February 9, just two days after receiving Emerson's trial report, Macdonald told Emerson that he was considering the Royal Prerogative of Mercy in the Beaton case. Emerson replied by letter immediately:

> Dear Sir Gordon,
> I beg to acknowledge receipt of your letter of today's date in reference to the case of Alfred Beaton, and the question of the exercise of the Royal Prerogative.
> Once we eliminate the defence of drunkenness and

insanity we are inevitably driven to the conclusion that this murder was committed in a state of ungoverned, as distinct from ungovernable, rage possibly accentuated to some extent by alcohol. If the accused was a man of say, twenty-five or more, it would be my view that there are no circumstances which would justify the exercise of the Royal Prerogative.

We cannot, however, discard entirely the fact that he is only a boy of nineteen, with very little schooling and certainly with no education. These factors can be urged in his favour. These are all the facts which are before me. There are others, however, which you are probably having examined, namely the family history and the general background of the accused. You will probably find from such enquiries that there are further grounds which should be considered in the prisoner's favour.

I am sorry I cannot be more helpful but you will understand I only have before me the evidence given during the trial. If you would care to discuss the matter with me I should be glad to go up and see you.

Yours Sincerely,
(Signed) L.E. Emerson

On February 8, the Commissioner of Justice requested a summary of Beaton's family history from Gillingham in Norris Arm. Gillingham, however, ran into unexpected hostility in gathering information from individuals in the community. Just as in St. John's, people in Norris Arm reacted with outrage over the death sentence. "It was found useless to attempt seeking information regarding Beaton," said Gillingham, "as the people of the place were so indignant over the sentence that hard language and lies were rife." He complained that people who had been in dire fear of Beaton when he was home were now in sympathy with him.

Gillingham indicated he was able to talk to Alfred's father, Frank Beaton. He outlined what Frank had told him about his son:

From the time that Alfred was a youth of about fifteen years, he was distant towards his family and would not

mix with them. He possessed a very bad and quick temper when provoked ... At the time of his mother's death,
some two years ago, Alfred Beaton did not break down,
as did the other children, but did appear very hurt. From
the time of his mother's death onwards he mixed even
less with the family. Mr. Beaton also stated that he would
take the children out in the boat on Sundays for a pic-
nic to try and ease their minds of their mother's death
but that Alfred would never go. Alfred did drink and
on these occasions he was possessed of a very dirty and
mean mood and temper.

Gillingham also reported that Beaton came from a clean and comfortable
home and the whole family was respected in the community. Beaton,
however, seemed to have run with the wrong crowd, a bunch of "roughs
and rowdies who live to drink and fight among themselves."

Gillingham attached incident reports describing Beaton's brushes
with the law which had been filed by Rangers Ledrew and Flight, who
had preceded him in 1947 and 1948 at the detachment in Norris Arm.
Gillingham expressed his frustration that "it [was] useless to try and get
true evidence at the present time due to the feelings that exist throughout
the community."

As the unfolding drama neared a climax, Gillingham's report contained the last details needed by the inner circle of government. On February 11, 1949, for the second time in seven years, the most powerful
men in the land met to determine the fate of a man sentenced to death
for murder. The faces had changed entirely since 1942. Sir Albert Walsh
was Commissioner of Justice, Herbert Pottle for Home Affairs and Education, Herman Quinton for Health and Welfare, R.L. James for Finance,
J.S. Neill for Public Utilities, and W.H. Flinn for Natural Resources. Governor Macdonald chaired the meeting.

The decision, after a brief discussion, was not a difficult one, driven
in part by the real danger that a controversial execution would blacken
the celebration of union with Canada. The commissioners' decision in
the case of The King versus Alfred Beaton is contained in Minute #106-
49: "After consideration of all the circumstances in connection with the
case it was decided to advise His Excellency, the Governor, to exercise the

Royal Prerogative and commute to life imprisonment the death sentence passed upon the prisoner."

Under different circumstances, the headline story in the February 12 weekend edition of the *Evening Telegram* should have been the news out of Ottawa that the House of Commons had given third reading to a bill approving the Terms of Union between Canada and Newfoundland. Only the formality of a senate vote and royal approval remained for Confederation to be complete. The story was relegated to second place by the dramatic announcement from the Department of Justice.

"BEATON WILL NOT HANG," screamed the banner headline across the front page of the Saturday papers. The communique published underneath the headline outlined the special powers of the "Governor and Commander-in-Chief of the Island of Newfoundland and its Dependencies" to extend or to withhold a pardon or reprieve to any person sentenced to death "within our said Island." The governor could exercise this power in consultation with the six commissioners, but in the end he could make his decision "according to his own deliberate judgement":

> His Excellency the Governor has complied with these instructions and has sought and obtained the advice of the Commission. His Excellency has, in this case, decided to exercise his prerogative and directs that the sentence of death imposed on Alfred Beaton on Friday, February 4, 1949 for the murder of Dorothea Manuel, be commuted to one of life imprisonment, the case to be reviewed by the appropriate authorities, at a date not later than ten years from the date of sentence and thereafter at intervals not exceeding three years.

City and regional papers applauded the decision and devoted editorial space to the story the following week. On Monday, the *Daily News* noted that "His Excellency the Governor had expressed the public wish. The death sentence had sent a shudder through the community ..."

An editorial in the February 19 edition of the *Grand Falls Advertiser* stated that the case had aroused widespread discussion on the morality of the death penalty; "many found the extreme penalty of the law too harshly unmerciful." While expressing sympathy for the family of the victim, the editor voiced the opinion that taking another life in vengeance would not bring comfort to her sorrowing relatives.

The editor of the *Twillingate Sun* expressed similar sentiments on February 19. "Judging by opinion published in a number of local papers and from the man on the street," said the editor, "the Governor has expressed the public wish."

In the same edition, the paper informed its readers that when Alfred Beaton learned from his legal counsel that his sentence had been commuted to life imprisonment, he appeared quite relieved "but [was] somewhat brief in conversation." When he was also told that 10,000 citizens of St. John's had signed petitions to have his death sentence commuted, Beaton was reported to have said, "Yes, sir. It's very good. They must be very nice people."

Eight

The past is never dead ...
—William Faulkner

With the date for confederation rapidly approaching, Sir Gordon Macdonald, Newfoundland's last colonial governor, made preparations for his departure. On Saturday, March 5, 1949, he took to the airwaves to say goodbye to the thousands of people he had met over his three years in office. It was a speech designed to foster unity and to heal the wounds opened in the often bitter and divisive debate over the political future of Newfoundland and Labrador:

> The task of building a better and brighter Newfoundland will be difficult, but I am not prepared to believe it impossible. I am not prepared to believe it is beyond the capacity of the people of this country to find the ways and means of performing such a task, formidable though it be. It can be done. It must be done. In fact I have sufficient confidence to say it will be done.

Macdonald repeated, as he had done many times during his visits along the coast of Newfoundland and Labrador, that the challenge was not just for men. At a time when women were not seen in public and professional life, he felt strongly that they must take their rightful place in society:

> The need is for men and women of fine and noble spirit. We need of course, men and women of wide experience and clear vision, men and women accustomed to handling big undertakings. Newfoundland needs, indeed she cannot cope with the problems of the future without men and women possessing such qualities.

Some listeners must have wondered whether it was the wisdom and voice of Portia.

The next day, a sunny Sunday morning, several hundred well-wishers gathered on the waterfront as Macdonald and his family participated in a simple ceremony to express their official goodbyes to military and civilian officials in the city before boarding their passenger ship to England. C.J. Burchell, the High Commissioner for Canada, was in attendance as were Emerson, Sir Leonard Outerbridge, and the Lord Bishop of Newfoundland. The Macdonald party boarded:

> Bedecked with colorful flags fluttering in a mild northeast breeze, the R.M.S. *Nova Scotia* pulled slowly away from her moorings at the Furness Withy pier … carrying with her to England, Newfoundland's last English appointed governor, His Excellency Sir Gordon Macdonald, K.C.M.G., Lady Macdonald and his family.

As the ship moved into mid-stream the governor and his family waved from the captain's deck. A reporter from the *Daily News* observed that Lady Macdonald appeared to be weeping.

Before his departure, Macdonald had recommended a number of Newfoundlanders for King's Honours, the most prominent of whom was Ranger Gillingham of Norris Arm. On March 26, the *Royal Gazette* printed the announcement that King George VI was pleased to award the King's Police and Fire Services Medal for Gallantry to no. 107, Ranger First Class, Eric Bruce Gillingham of the Newfoundland Rangers.

The *Twillingate Sun*, which carried the story on April 2, noted that the award recognized "the exceptional courage shown by [Gillingham] in disarming and apprehending at the immediate risk of his own life, one Alfred Beaton of Norris Arm, on October last." It was the second time in the short history of the Newfoundland Rangers that one of its officers had received the medal for gallantry.

Throughout March 1949, a Newfoundland delegation chaired by Sir Albert Walsh worked on the final details of the Terms of Union in Ottawa. The delegation included such notables as Joey Smallwood, Gordon Bradley, and Ches Crosbie. The final legal hurdle was cleared on March

23 when the British government granted Royal Assent to the amended British North America Act, allowing for the union between Canada and Newfoundland.

On March 31, Emerson chaired the last meeting of the Commission of Government in the judges' chambers of the Supreme Court on Duckworth Street. The next day Newfoundland was welcomed into the Canadian federation. The laws of Canada, including the Canadian Criminal Code, replaced the laws of Newfoundland.

To jump-start the new government, Emerson presided at the swearing-in ceremony of Newfoundland's first lieutenant governor, Sir Albert Walsh, who did not want the job but agreed to take on the role on a temporary basis. Other events were to shorten his term considerably.

Late in the day on May 19, 1949, the citizens of St. John's learned that Emerson had been stricken just before noon with a heart attack and died shortly after at St. Clare's Mercy Hospital. Only a week earlier he had celebrated his 59th birthday. His death shocked the justice system which he had dominated for so many years.

Tributes to Emerson appeared in the press the next day. The *Daily News* remarked on his lengthy career in public life, "the most momentous occasion being the swearing in of the first Lieutenant Governor of the new province." The paper highlighted his skills in the courtroom: "his summations of evidence were candid, definite and unambiguous, his knowledge of the law profound."

The legal community gathered at the Supreme Court Building for a special memorial ceremony on the afternoon of May 20. Justice Brian Dunfield offered a glowing tribute to his colleague:

> The late Chief Justice, Sir Lewis Edward Emerson came of a long list of forbears eminent in the profession in this island and did full credit to his ancestry. He was a first class lawyer in the technical sense. While his impartiality, his care in sentencing and his disposition towards mercy rather than severity, especially in cases affecting the young, were all that they should be, as we, his colleagues know better than anyone else.

Many outside the legal profession took issue with the words but on such a solemn occasion their thoughts were left unstated.

With the death of Emerson, the government of Canada began its search for a new chief justice in Newfoundland. On September 5, 1949, Walsh vacated the office of lieutenant governor and accepted the position.

In the summer of 1951 the Canadian government announced that the royal couple, Princess Elizabeth and Prince Philip, would visit Newfoundland as part of their Canadian tour. The visit was scheduled for November 11 and 12. Isaac Mercer of Mercer, Mifflin, and O'Dea thought it would be the right time to test the waters for a pardon for their client, Alfred Beaton, who had fulfilled two years of his life sentence for murder. Mercer made a formal request for pardon to the Hon. Leslie R. Curtis, Minister of Justice and attorney general on October 8.

Mercer reminded the minister that, under the terms of Beaton's imprisonment, the case could be reviewed at a date not later than 10 years from the date of the sentence and after that time the case should be reviewed every three years. This certainly left open the possibility of a pardon, reasoned Mercer, and he outlined his case to Curtis:

> Alfred Beaton has been confined to His Majesty's Penitentiary since February 4, 1949. The writer has conversed with Mr. Case, the superintendent of His Majesty's Penitentiary and I understand that Alfred Beaton has been a model prisoner and that his behaviour has been exemplary in every way.... [W]e submit on behalf of Alfred Beaton, that the occasion of the visit of Her Royal Highness, Princess Elizabeth, and His Royal Highness, Prince Philip, would be a very appropriate time for the review to take place and if the authorities are satisfied with his conduct then Alfred Beaton might be pardoned.

The Minister of Justice reviewed the case and decided that Beaton did not meet the requirements outlined in Section 69 of the Canada Act respecting the conditional release of convicts from a penitentiary. Beaton had simply not served enough time in prison.

Alfred Beaton continued to be a model prisoner in the years ahead. By mid-1953 Superintendent Case was confident that Beaton could be moved to a minimum security facility. In a telephone conversation with Curtis on June 23, 1953, Case reviewed Beaton's progress and the two men agreed on the next step in rehabilitation. Case followed up with a formal request in writing:

> As per our telephone conversation of June 23 respecting the transfer of Alfred Beaton to the prison camp for a period of two or three months I wish to state ... Beaton's conduct has been exemplary in every respect. He has worked assisting the store-keeper, and attending school and has made good progress. In view of his conduct and trustworthiness, I have no hesitation in recommending he be transferred to the Prison Camp [at Salmonier] until the reopening of school in September. I do not feel there will be any attempt to escape, or other misconduct on his part while there, and feel that his conduct ... at the Prison Camp ... will be very material to the authorities when reviewing his case. Beaton is now twenty-four years old, having been nineteen when admitted.

The Minister of Justice approved the recommendation. Over the next six years Beaton remained a model prisoner. On December 22, 1959, he was released on parole from Her Majesty's Penitentiary after serving 11 years of his sentence. He relocated to another part of the province and did not re-offend. He died in 2015 at the age of 86.

The arrival of Gordon Macdonald as governor of Newfoundland in 1946 alone might have saved Alfred Beaton from the executioner, but the sudden awakening of public opinion against the death penalty during the momentous first week of February 1949 ensured that he would not hang.

Despite the considerable evidence of mental illness, and a strong recommendation for mercy, Herb Spratt had experienced no such luck. His execution on a sunny May morning in 1942 was the last in Newfoundland.

With the passage of time, the collective memory of the events within the justice system in Newfoundland during the 1940s faded into history.

For some, however, the memories would not die. The families and extended families of both the victims and the violent offenders became the invisible ones. For them there was to be no closure.

The brutal murder of Josephine O'Brien left her community in shock and her family devastated. William and Bridget O'Brien's grief for their lost daughter returned every year on the anniversary of her death. Every year they retired to their bedroom on St. Patrick's eve and did not emerge until the morning after St. Patrick's Day. With the passing years, Josephine's brothers and sisters buried the pain of her loss in a deepening silence. No one forgot the tragic events of March 17, 1942.

The O'Brien family did not support the death penalty imposed on Herb Spratt. For them, the execution compounded the tragedy. The family viewed the crime through the lens of mental illness, which should have resulted in Herb's transfer to the Hospital for Mental and Nervous Diseases. They did not seek vengeance.

For the Spratt family, the horror of Josephine's murder and the execution of Herb also left deep scars. For many months after the traumatic events in the spring of 1942, James Spratt did not attend routine meetings of City Council. By July, when he returned to regular attendance he was a changed man. His old energy had been drained and he found it difficult to participate in debates.

It took three years for Spratt to rediscover his passion for politics. His constituents encouraged him to run again for his seat on City Council. In the elections of November 1945, he finished first in the polls and was consequently appointed deputy mayor.

In May 1949, Spratt's good friend, Joseph R. Smallwood, encouraged him to run for the Newfoundland House of Assembly in the District of St. John's West as a candidate for the Liberal Party. Spratt easily won the seat and the new premier appointed him to Cabinet as Minister of Provincial Affairs, a post he held for two years before retiring from politics altogether.

But life would never be the same for Spratt. A random event like a picture of a gallows in a newspaper would set off a bout of depression. Annie Spratt grieved in silence for a lost son whom she loved unconditionally.

In Norris Arm the impact was no less severe. Beaton's deadly rampage on October 23, 1948, shattered the peace of the quiet community near the mouth of the Exploits River. In the aftermath, the Budgell family, particularly Dorothea's mother, was numbed by grief. Mrs. Budgell took on the responsibility for raising Dorothea's two young children. The decision to care for her grandchildren along with her faith and the support of her church enabled her to regain a sense of purpose in her life.

Hallett Manuel, Dorothea's husband, eventually overcame his loss and remarried.

After nearly 70 years there are still a few in Norris Arm who vividly recall that terrible Saturday night in 1948. For them the memories will not die.

Elsewhere in Canada, capital punishment continued until 1962. Just before Christmas of that year, Arthur Lucas and Ronald Turpin died at the end of a rope at the Don Jail in Toronto. Lucas was very likely innocent.

Only two other death sentences were handed down in the Supreme Court of Newfoundland, both in 1965. But by that time the Canadian government, as a matter of policy, was commuting all death sentences to life imprisonment. Capital punishment was in effect eliminated in Canada with the passing of Bill C-84 by the House of Commons in 1976.

Over the years, public opinion has wavered but successive national polls have shown a steady decline in support for the ultimate penalty. In Newfoundland and Labrador public support for the death penalty stands at 17 per cent, the lowest in the country.

Bibliography

Primary Sources

The Rooms, Provincial Archives of Newfoundland and Labrador:

Correspondence of the Commission of Government, GN38, Box S4-3-1.

Minutes, Commission of Government, GN13/1/8.

Ranger Force Reports, 1945–1947, File 32, Box S2-5-2.

The King vs. Alfred Beaton, GN13, Box 148.

The Supreme Court of Newfoundland and Labrador:

Witness Depositions, Central District Court, St. John's, March 30–April 4, 1942.

The King vs. Herbert Augustus Spratt transcripts, April 27–28, 1942.

Witness Depositions, Central District Court, Grand Falls, December 2–4, 1948.

The King vs Alfred Beaton transcripts, File 1948-0477.

Notice of Appeal: The King vs. Alfred Beaton, February 12, 1949.

Newspapers and Other Periodicals

Atlantic Guardian, 1948–49

The British Colonist, 1861

Evening Telegram, 1939–49

Daily News, 1939–49

Grand Falls Advertiser, 1947–49

Twillingate Sun, 1948–49

Online Sources

Anonymous. 2010. HMS *Rodney* and the Sinking of the *Bismarck*. http://www.benidog.co.uk/Recollections/Rodney%20Bismarck.html

Debates: British House of Lords, volumes 165–169. Hansard 1803–2005. http://www.hansard.millbanksystems.com/lords/1950/.

Gadboury, Lorraine and Antonio Lechasseur. Persons Sentenced to Death in Canada, 1867–1976.

An inventory of case files in the Department of Justice. Government Archives Division. National Archives of Canada. 1994. data2.archives.ca/pdf/pdf001/p000001052.pdf.

Hollett, Ed. The Sir Robert Bond Papers, 2010. http://bondpapers.blogspot.ca/2013/02/letters-patent-1934.html

Jones, Frank. The Carelton County Man Who Was Hung Twice, Benny Swimm, February 7, 1981. http://www.rootsweb.ancestry.com/~nbcarlet/hanging.htm

The M'Naghten Rule. 2015. http://www.criminal.findlaw.com/criminal-procedure/.

Queensland Law Review Commission. A Review of the Excuse of Accident and the Defence of Provocation. Report no. 64. September 2008. http://www.gld.gov.au.

Tomlinson, Ashley. Capital Punishment in Great Britain: Theories Concerning Abolition. 2006. http://www.eiu.edu/historia/archives/Tomlinson.pdf.

Turrell, Rob. It's a Mystery: The Royal Prerogative of Mercy in England, Canada and South Africa. 2000. http://www.chs.revues.org/index850.html.

Other Print Sources

Documents from the O'Brien family collection.

Correspondence with Hon. Susan Stride, granddaughter of Sir Gordon Macdonald.

Secondary Sources

Anderson, Frank W. *Hanging in Canada: A Concise History of Capital Punishment*. Calgary: A Frontier Publication, 1973.

Butts, Edward. *Running with Dillinger: The Story of Red Hamilton and Other Forgotten Canadian Outlaws*. Toronto: Dundern Press, 2008.

Butts, Edward. *Murder: Twelve True Stories of Homicide in Canada*. Toronto: Dundern Press, 2011.

Chardavoyne, David G. *A Hanging in Detroit: Stephen Gifford Simmons and the Last Execution under Michigan Law*. Detroit: Wayne State University, 2003.

Duff, Charles. *A Handbook of Hanging*. New York: The New York Review of Books, 2001.

Eddleston, John J. *The Encyclopaedia of Executions*. London: John Blake Publishing Ltd., 2004.

Fielding, Steve. *The Executioner's Bible: The Story of Every British Hangman of the Twentieth Century*. London: John Blake Publishing Ltd., 2007.

Fielding, Steve. *Pierrepoint: A Family of Executioners: The Story of Britain's Infamous Hangmen*. London: John Blake Publishing Ltd., 2008.

Greenwood, F. Murray and Beverley Boissery. *Uncertain Justice: Canadian Women and Capital Punishment 1754–1953*. Toronto: Dundern Press, 2000.

High, Steven, ed. *Occupied St. John's: A Social History of a City at War, 1939–1945*. Montreal: McGill-Queen's University Press, 2010.

Hornby, Jim. *In the Shadow of the Gallows: Criminal Law and Capital Punishment in Prince Edward Island, 1769–1941*. Summerside, PEI: Williams & Crue Ltd., 1998.

Horwood, Harold. *A History of the Newfoundland Ranger Force*. St. John's: Breakwater Books Ltd., 1986.

Hoshowsky, Robert J. *The Last to Die: Ronald Turpin, Arthur Lucas, and the End of Capital Punishment in Canada*. Toronto: Dundern Press, 2007.

Hustak, Alan. *They Were Hanged*. Toronto: James Lorimer & Company Publishers, 1987.

Leyton-Brown, Ken. *The Practice of Execution in Canada*. Vancouver: UBC Press, 2010.

McGrath, Darrin, Robert Smith, Ches Parsons, and Norman Crane. *The Newfoundland Rangers*. St. John's: DRC Publishing, 2005.

Neary, Peter, ed. *White Tie and Decorations: Sir John and Lady Hope Simpson in Newfoundland, 1934–1936*. Toronto, Buffalo, London: University of Toronto Press, 1997.

Nicholson, G.W.L. *The Fighting Newfoundlander: A History of the Royal Newfoundland Regiment*. Montreal and Kingston: McGill-Queen's University Press, 2006.

Nugent, John C., ed. *The End of Sacrifice: The Capital Punishment Writings of John Howard Yoder*. Harrisonburg, VA: Herald Press, 2011.

O'Flaherty, Patrick. *Leaving the Past Behind: Newfoundland History from 1934*. St. John's: Long Beach Press, 2011.

Pickett, Carrol. *Within These Walls: Memoirs of a Death House Chaplain*. New York: St. Martin's Press, 2002.

Potter-Efron, Ronald T. *Rage: A Step by Step Guide to Overcoming Explosive Anger*. Oakland, CA: New Harbinger Publications, 2007.

Prejean, Helen. *Dead Man Walking*. New York: Random House, 1993.

Sellin, Thorsten. *The Penalty of Death*. Thousand Oaks, CA: Sage Publications Inc., 2013.

Ward, H. Snowden, ed. *My Experiences as an Executioner: James Berry*. London: Percy Lund & Co., 1918.

Winchester, Simon. *The Professor and the Madman: A Tale of Murder, Insanity and the Making of the Oxford English Dictionary*. New York: Harper Collins, 1998.